PERSPECTIVES ON

SOVIET JEWRY

PERSPECTIVES ON

SOVIET JEWRY

NATHAN GLAZER

MOSHE DECTER

WILLIAM KOREY

JOHN A. ARMSTRONG

ALEX INKELES

HANS J. MORGENTHAU

MAURICE FRIEDBERG

PAUL LENDVAI

Academic Committee on Soviet Jewry
and
The Anti-Defamation League of B'nai B'rith

Published for

ANTI - DEFAMATION LEAGUE OF B'NAI B'RITH
315 LEXINGTON AVENUE
NEW YORK, NEW YORK 10016

by

KTAV PUBLISHING HOUSE, INC.
NEW YORK, NEW YORK 10002

SBN 87068-167-2

MANUFACTURED IN THE UNITED STATES OF AMERICA

Contents

John A. Armstrong is Professor of Political Science at the University of Wisconsin and former president of the American Association for the Advancement of Slavic Studies

Moshe Decter is Director of Jewish Minorities Research specializing in problems of the Jews in Eastern Europe and the U.S.S.R. He is also executive director of the Conference on the Status of Soviet Jews and a consultant to the Academic Committee on Soviet Jewry

Maurice Friedberg is Professor of Slavic Languages and Literatures and Director of the Russian and East European Institute at Indiana University

Nathan Glazer is Professor of Education and Social Structure at the Harvard University Graduate School of Education, former Professor of Sociology at the University of California, Berkeley and past Chairman of the Academic Committee on Soviet Jewry

Alex Inkeles is Professor of Sociology at Harvard University and an Associate of the Harvard Russian Research Center

William Korey is Director of the United Nations Office of the B'nai B'rith International Council, former member of the faculty at Columbia University and the City College of New York and Visiting Professor of Russian History at Yeshiva University

Paul Lendvai is a Hungarian-born Austrian political writer who is personally acquainted with some of the history he relates. He has visited the East European nations regularly.

Hans J. Morgenthau, International Relations specialist and political philosopher, holds chairs in Political Science at the University of Chicago and the City University of New York. He is Chairman of the Academic Committee on Soviet Jewry

INTRODUCTION

IT is never easy to get attention for a problem of the second, or third, order of importance. In a world in which the horrors of the Vietnam war continue, in which nuclear destruction still threatens, in which the environment deteriorates, it is not easy to make a claim for the problems of the Jews of Soviet Russia. We cannot cry "genocide," and even spiritual genocide, which is a truer characterization of what is going on in Soviet Russia, would strike some of us as excessively shrill and propagandistic. Yet what is going on is bad enough, and in the two years since the articles in this book were written (they were initially delivered at a Conference of the Academic Committee for Soviet Jewry, held in Washington, May 11-12, 1969, and have been revised for this second edition),* it has become considerably worse. As I write, two young Jewish men who have been tried for plotting to hijack a plane to get out of the country stand condemned to death. The widespread outcry against the ferocity of this sentence prevented their execution.

Some of the background facts are set forth in the first two papers: Dr. Korey reports on the exaggerated and vicious campaign against "Zionism" which has raged in the Soviet press — and its serious reverberations, first in Poland, then in Czechoslovakia — for the last three years. Of course this might be explained as simply the domestic expression of Russian foreign policy which, in its support of the Arab position, will naturally denounce those who support what is viewed as an enemy state. But those of us who recall campaigns against "rootless cosmopolitans," " 'Joint' agents," "financial exploiters," know that in whatever social role Jews present themselves in the Soviet Union — as nationalists or anti-nationalists, religious or anti-religious, small-scale tradesmen or large-scale bureaucrats —

---

* Ed.: In addition to the conference papers presented in this book, two recent articles have also been added — "The Terror that Fails: A Report on the Arrests and Trial of Soviet Jews" by Moshe Decter, and "Moscow — Center and Exporter of Anti-Semitism" by Paul Lendvai.

they are peculiarly subject in Soviet Russia to suspicion, ridicule, criticism, denunciation. And the special social and political structure of the Soviet Union—in which nothing appears in print or in the mass media that does not in some sense bear the approval of overwhelmingly powerful state authorities—inevitably must lead us to give this more attention than might similar ranting in this, very different, country.

We are concerned with more than the atmosphere of anti-Semitism, with the covert encouragement that it regularly receives from the state-controlled mass media. We are concerned with what it means for Russian Jews to live in this atmosphere of suspicion, ridicule, denunciation. It is clear from the many conversations between visitors to Russia and Russian Jews that many feel the force of such an atmosphere, leading to circumspection, fear, painful choices when the individual Russian Jew decides how much of a Jew—and in what way—he dares to be.

We are concerned too with the actual restriction of the opportunities of Jews. In the practical spheres of life, they have for twenty years or more found various branches of public service and professional activity restricted. How far this restriction extends it is hard to say—Russia is not an open society. But Jews in Russia are aware of it. The counts by Soviet experts of officers in the Foreign Service, the armed services, of Russian scholars going abroad, all suggest this restriction is severe.

We are concerned with the almost total ban on any form of Jewish cultural or communal expression—the almost total absence of Jewish schools, except for a miniscule and decaying Rabbinical seminary, the absence of teaching materials in Yiddish and Hebrew, the failure to print Hebrew Bibles, the refusal to countenance more than one Jewish publication for a community of three million, the severe restrictions on religious observance, the drying up of the forms of Jewish expression, whether in Hebrew, Yiddish, or Russian. The carefully doled out reprinting of occasional Yiddish classics is no substitute for the rich Jewish life—radically restricted as it was politically by the Communist government—that existed until 1949, and was then brutally, and before its time, cut off.

Finally, we are concerned about that ultimate limitation in freedom that afflicts Russian Jews as it afflicts all Soviet citizens—the freedom to leave, and to search for a better life elsewhere.

THERE has been intense argument as to whether the present barely flickering expressions of Jewish life in the Soviet Union reflect the simple force of assimilation, reducing the desire of Russian Jews to express themselves through the antique forms of the Jewish religion, or the more modern forms of

Jewish and Hebrew cultural expression. Moshe Decter's paper gives to my mind a powerful analysis of the varieties of Jewish communities and Jewish experience in the Soviet Union. It seems scarcely conceivable to him that the second largest Jewish community in the world — next to that of the United States — should not want to express its Jewish interests in more than the few pallid instruments made available by the Russian state. I think no objective reader of his analysis will accept easily the apology of Soviet authorities that these few last remnants of Jewish expression are all that the Russian Jews are willing to continue.

I have suggested that it is hard to maintain interest, in a world of horrors, in a problem of less urgency. It is of course a matter of great urgency to those of us concerned for the Jewish people, since Soviet Jewry is the second largest Jewish community in the world. The conditions of its life, its ability to express itself and regenerate itself, is a matter of the highest priority, second only to that of the survival of the Jewish nation in the Middle East. One reason why it is hard to maintain interest in the second problem is that we are all at a loss when we consider the mystifying question of how public opinion in the United States — and elsewhere in the Western World — can influence the leaders and rulers of Soviet Russia, a nation that is so mysterious to us that even the question of how its *own* public opinion influences its policies remains obscure. Even before we know how the public opinion of groups in the United States might influence the Soviet government to take a more generous stance toward the Jewish population, we would have to understand — and again this is mysterious — why there exists this persistent and protean streak of anti-Semitism running through Soviet policy. The three presentations by Professors Armstrong, Inkeles and Morgenthau throw a good deal of light on both questions — the sources of anti-Jewish trends in Soviet policy, and the question of whether opinion in another nation can possibly influence policy on such an internal, domestic matter. On this latter question, there are truly helpful suggestions and analyses — and the answer seems clear that, aside from the simple demands of conscience which would prevent us from remaining silent in the face of governmental injustice to Soviet Jews, there is at least some hope that an informed and aroused public opinion, vigilant to the situation of Soviet Jews and the actions of the Soviet government, may have some influence upon it.

There is a sense, even for those who may not have a primary concern for the future of the Jewish people, in which the situation of the Jews of Soviet Russia is not a second problem, second to others. We become increasingly aware that the problem of the twentieth century, and the problem of the twenty-first century too, is that of maintaining a world in which different national traditions, different group orientations, may survive, and one in which a range of different ethnic and racial groups will be able to find social and political forms that do permit them to live and flourish together. We are all aware of W.E.B. DuBois' prophetic statement, "the problem of the twentieth century is the problem of the color line." When French-speaking Canadians riot against a bill to protect teaching in English, when Malayans riot against Chinese, when Belgium is almost severed by the conflict between Fleming and Walloon, when Kikuyu and Luo square off in Kenya in a struggle that may yet become as grave as that in Nigeria, when Protestant and Catholic struggle in Northern Ireland, we see we must expand DuBois's statement—the problem is not only the color line but all the lines that divide racial groups, tribal groups, ethnic groups, religious groups—all groups that see themselves as in some way distinct, bearing an ancient tradition and trying to maintain that tradition in the future. From this point of view, the fate of the Jews in Soviet Russia is part of a complex world-wide issue, that of the survival of groups of different cultural character in modern societies and that of the viable relationships in modern societies of such groups.

Marxists were never so wrong as when they failed to recognize how powerful were the drives that connected people to such groups and how much meaning they gave to those identified with them. J. L. Talmon, the Israeli historian, writes: "One of Rosa Luxemburg's letters from prison to a Jewish friend [says]: 'Why do you pester me with your Jewish sorrow? There is no room in my heart for the Jewish troubles.' And she goes on to speak most eloquently of the Chinese coolies and of the Bantus in South Africa. Twenty-five years later, after the Germans had occupied it, there was not a single Jew left alive in Rosa's native Zamosc."

I do not quote this passage because I expect any such fate for the Jews of Russia but only to remind those for whom there is no room in their hearts for Jewish troubles that Jewish troubles have never been Jewish troubles alone, and least so today.

NATHAN GLAZER

JEWISH NATIONAL CONSCIOUSNESS IN THE SOVIET UNION

MOSHE DECTER

IF there is any logic to history — that is, if it is possible to speak of causes and effects and of reasonable expectations — then the survival of the Jewish people has no part of it. There is no precedent or parallel in Western history to the persistence of the Jews through the centuries and millenia.

Is it "logical" or "reasonable" to expect that a people whose political independence was shattered and whose religious insitutions were destroyed, a people who were thereafter exiled from their homeland and dispersed throughout the world, then subjected in the course of twenty centuries to every conceivable form of degradation and humiliation, assault and mass murder in virtually every segment of the globe — is it logical to expect that this people should have survived, even thrived, in creativity and dignity? Even to have passed through the purgatory of the greatest holocaust in the history of man's bestiality, and to have then gone on to restore to life their ancient homeland?

Clearly, the Jews are a perverse and obdurate people. Categories of social science and historiography can doubtless be applied to explain rationally the causes and circumstances of this strange phenomenon. Yet there will remain an inexplicable core, a residual element of mystery.

Similar considerations may pertain to the Jews of the USSR. For more than half a century, these millions of Jews have lived through

[9]

one shattering experience after another, all calculated to augur the demise of Jewish national consciousness and thus of a self-aware Jewish group. The logic of history would seem to dictate the imminent disappearance of Soviet Jewry. It is relevant to our inquiry here to outline the unfolding of that logic.

The very ideological underpinnings of the Bolshevik regime established a context and created an atmosphere entirely hostile to the perpetuation of a viable Jewish community. For Lenin, the Jews were a historical anachronism and Judaism an intellectual excrescence. He and his colleagues believed that the Jews had no national character of their own, that they persisted as a group (and thus perpetuated outmoded customs and dangerous superstitions) solely because of the external pressures of anti-Semitism and other evils perpetrated by capitalism. Destroy the system, remove the shackles that bound the Jews, and they would swiftly disappear as a recognizable entity, moving as individuals into the mainstream of Russian life.

It should be noted at this point that it was the democratic revolution of February 1917 that emancipated the Jews, abolished the Pale of Settlement, eliminated all forms of discrimination and removed the official bar to their participation in every facet of the new revolutionary life. All this was perpetuated by the Bolsheviks, who were firmly and explicitly opposed to anti-Semitism.

At the same time, the Bolsheviks undertook the systematic elimination of all aspects and forms of Jewish life which conflicted or competed (or were thought to do so) with the new system and its ideology. It began with the massive repression of every element of religious life that had traditionally characterized Russian Jewry — synagogues, yeshivot, religious schools, books and publications, etc. This was, of course, part and parcel of a broader, general anti-religious policy and was by no means restricted to the Jews, nor motivated by any hostility to Jews as such. Still, it struck a decisive blow at Jewish communal life and national consciousness.

But, though most Jews remained religious, Judaism was not the only, nor perhaps even the main, competitor of Bolshevism, and not the sole Jewish victim of its inexorable monopolistic drive. For — characteristic anomaly of Jewish history — in the half-century before the October Revolution, alongside and despite the pauperization and persecution engendered by oppressive Tsarist policy, Jewish national-cultural life was experiencing a tremendous renascence.

This was the period when Hebrew, the ancient language of prayer and study, blossomed forth into a modern language. This development was paralleled by the no less extraordinary transformation of Yiddish from the spoken tongue of the masses into a sophisticated literary language. In both languages, significant literatures, including instances of world rank, were being created.

There was an important Jewish labor and democratic socialist movement led by residues of the Bund on Russian soil. There was a burgeoning Hebrew theatre. There was a thriving and constantly expanding world of publication, with innumerable newspapers and periodicals and hundreds and thousands of Jewish books published in Yiddish, Hebrew and even Russian. There were many secular Hebrew and Yiddish schools. There was a multivariety of Jewish movements, institutions and organizations of every conceivable sort. There was, above all, a growing Zionist movement which had the support and sympathy of the vast majority of Russian Jews, and which imbued the renascence with moral, emotional and intellectual passion.

All this was ruthlessly destroyed by the Bolsheviks.

What unlimited prospects of cultural and intellectual creation stood before that numerous, explosive and richly endowed Russian Jewry in 1917! What a historic tragedy for the Jewish people was the subversion of those prospects, the loss of that future!

WHAT, then, of Jewish national consciousness after the Revolution? To put it simply, Russian Jewry was largely deprived of much of its intelligentsia, the element that gave character, impetus and direction to the group. One has here to distinguish broadly between two segments of that intelligentsia: the assimilating intelligentsia and the intrinsically Jewish intelligentsia.

Among the former are to be counted all those who played so substantial and influential a role in the leadership of the various radical movements even before the Revolution — among the Bolsheviks, Mensheviks, Social Revolutionaries; as well as those consciously Jewish radicals such as the left-wing Bundists and left-wing Socialist-Zionists who subsequently joined the Bolsheviks. Included also was the much larger number of fine young Jews, but recently emancipated, who responded to the promise of the Revolution and were swept up in the romantic enthusiasm it unleashed and the noble idealism it elicited.

The intrinsically Jewish intelligentsia was swiftly eliminated by the new regime. The rabbis and other religious leaders, teachers and scholars were either imprisoned or decimated. The hasidic movement was atomized and forced into a precarious underground existence. The Zionist leadership was also either imprisoned, liquidated or permitted to leave the country. Most of the Hebrew writers and thinkers, and many of the Yiddish writers left the country.

In short, Russian Jewry was largely bereft of a vital, autonomous intellectual leadership. And yet the Jewish masses remained for very long resistant to the Bolshevik assaults upon Judaism and Jewish consciousness. So much so that, after a few years, the authorities found it wise to establish Jewish cultural, educational and communal institutions (all in the Yiddish language exclusively) to meet irreducible needs—naturally, within rigorous and narrow political limits: professional repertory theatres, schools, publishing houses and newspapers and periodicals, departments of Jewish study and research in institutions of higher learning. But the levers of power and decision in this institutional framework were wielded by Jewish Communists who were dedicated to the identical objectives, in this area, as their non-Jewish comrades—the evisceration of Jewish national culture and its ultimate disappearance, along with the general assimilation of the Jews.

Even within so discouraging a context, however, a pleiad of Yiddish novelists, poets, critics and actor-directors was able to work fruitfully for some years. It is true that most of them had done their best work even before the Revolution and in the decade of the '20s. Still, they constituted the last remnant of an authentic Jewish intelligentsia—until their creative power and appeal were stifled, along with everybody else's, with the enthronement of Stalinolatry beginning in the late '30s, waxing during World War II, and reaching its apotheosis in the last six or seven years of the dictator's life.

But even this narrowly delimited institutional structure and weak intellectual leadership gradually began to lose their efficacy, beginning as early as the late 1930s, the period of the Great Purge. It was then that a new dimension was added to the traditional Soviet policy toward the Jews. That new dimension can only be described as crude anti-Semitism, and from its inception until its culmination in Stalin's last years its cutting edge was brought to bear concurrently against both the assimilating and the intrinsically Jewish intelligentsias.

THIS is not the place to detail the process, but a broad overview is necessary in order to understand how Soviet Jewry was utterly deprived of its intelligentsia, as well as the relation of that process to the state of Jewish national consciousness then and now.

In 1937, keen observers, including former Party members, could sense a rising hostility toward Jews, stemming from the prominence of Jewish Communists in the massively brutal purges which swept the country under Stalin's careful direction; the tyrant was far from averse to exploiting this form of popular resentment to deflect it from himself and to bolster his policy. In 1938 an attack began on Jewish culture. All Yiddish schools were closed between then and 1940. Not less significant was the closing of the Yiddish sections in the Bielorussian and Ukrainian Academies of Sciences. All research in Jewish subjects there was abruptly ended.

[12]

The Stalin-Hitler Pact of August 1939 introduced far-reaching new elements of anti-Semitism into Kremlin policy. Jews began systematically to be "discouraged" from seeking careers in the foreign ministry, and the elimination and exclusion of Jews gradually extended to every branch of government and party apparatus that dealt with foreigners and foreign affairs. The Jews were not to be trusted. Anecdotes are rife about the extent, depth and harshness of anti-Semitism in the Red Army during the War — both from the ranks below and from the officers above. After the war there began the steady policy of excluding Jews from all "security-sensitive" sectors of State and Party affairs.

In January 1948, Shlomo Mikhoels, the most distinguished Jew in the Soviet Union — star and director of the Jewish State Theatre *and* chairman of the Jewish Anti-Fascist Committee (created during the war to establish ties with world Jewry and enlist its support for the Soviet war effort) — was killed in a mysterious automobile accident. The event filled his comrades of the Jewish intelligentsia with vague foreboding, for they sensed it to be a political execution (confirmed by Soviet sources many years later) and so an evil omen for Jewish culture and the Jewish community.

Their foreboding was warranted. In the autumn of that year, all remaining Jewish cultural institutions — the Yiddish theatre, the publishing house, the lone newspaper, libraries — were liquidated; even the Jewish type-face was melted down! Thousands of Yiddish writers and cultural figures were arrested, imprisoned or simply disappeared in slave labor camps.

In January 1949 came the turn of the assimilating intelligentsia. In that month *Pravda* initiated the notorious "anti-cosmopolitan" campaign, as a consequence of which many thousands of Jews were purged, in the midst of a hysterical, thinly disguised anti-Semitic propaganda campaign, from leading positions in academic and artistic life and journalism. Jews were accused of being "rootless cosmopolitans," "aliens, without a motherland," "not indigenous," "incapable of understand true Russian patriotism," etc. On August 12, 1952, the two dozen most gifted and distinguished Jewish writers and cultural leaders were executed as spies and bourgeois nationalists. In November of the same year came the Moscow-inspired purge trial in Prague, one of the most anti-Semitic trials of the century, at which life-long dedicated Communists and fanatic Stalinists (like Rudolf Slansky, leader of the Czechoslovak party) were forced to confess to having been Zionists, bourgeois Jewish nationalists, traitors and spies all their lives.

This fantastic, ferocious campaign culminated in January 1953 with the announcement of a sensational plot by a group of doctors, mostly Jews, to assassinate the Soviet leadership at the behest of

American intelligence and the international Jewish bourgeoisie. A massive new purge seemed to be in the making, and the Jews were to bear the brunt of it. For them, those last five years of Stalin's life were what they called "the Black Years" and they regarded it as a miraculous chance that they were spared only by the death of the tyrant in March 1953.

This motif—of anti-Jewish suspicion, distrust, discrimination and exclusion—had long since supplanted internationalist assimilationism as the root of Soviet policy toward the Jews and has dominated that policy since Stalin's day. The heart of the matter is that the Jews are *ab initio* not regarded as indigenous; they are felt to be somehow not quite at home. At bottom, they are still thought of as aliens and strangers; the distinction between *we* and *they* is still deep and potent. Thus, Nikita Khrushchev, then the Soviet boss, could permit himself to say to a French socialist delegation that interviewed him in May 1956:

> Should the Jews want to occupy the foremost positions in *our* republic now, it would *naturally* be taken amiss by the *indigenous* inhabitants. The latter would not accept these *pretensions* at all well, especially since they do not consider themselves less intelligent or less capable than the Jews. Or, for instance, when a Jew in the Ukraine is appointed to an important post and *he surrounds himself with Jewish collaborators*, it is *understandable* that this should create jealousy and hostility toward the Jews. [*Emphasis added.*]

Thus the root of Soviet policy is distrust and suspicion of the Jew *qua* Jew, of the Jews as a recognizable entity, of the Jewish people as such—and of Soviet Jewry insofar as it consciously identifies with that people and its history and destiny. And so the objective of that policy is, through a process of gradual attrition and attenuation and within an ambience of barely concealed hostility, to eradicate every spoor of an identifiable and proudly self-aware Jewish group. From this flows all else—all the deprivations, all the discriminations, all the large and small slights and silences, and the surrealistic and irrational propaganda about Judaism and Israel.

SO the future of this richly endowed community is placed in jeopardy. Cut off from its past, atomized from within, isolated from its people abroad, bereft of educational institutions and publications, subjected to a wide range of discriminatory deprivations, the Soviet Jewish community is denied its natural right of group existence and meaningful identity. Jewish national consciousness—according to the logic of history—would appear to be at low ebb.

Thus it is with a certain plausibility that Soviet spokesmen can maintain that, after more than half a century of Communist rule, the

Jews in the Soviet Union have become assimilated linguistically, culturally, intellectually.

As for religion, the USSR is an atheist country. Go into the synagogues, says the Soviet argument, and see for yourself. On most days you will barely find a quorum for prayer. And on Sabbaths and holidays you will find very few or no young people. It is only the old-timers whom one will encounter there.

And as for secular Jewish culture, the Jews are just not interested anymore. Young Soviet Jews in particular think of themselves as part of the greater Russian and Soviet culture and society.

Indeed, the American, especially the American Jew, concerned with this problem will find such reasoning hard to deny. If he has visited the USSR he will have discovered for himself the apparent accuracy of the Soviet apologetics: No interest, and therefore no need for institutions and education.

In any event, the American will naturally tend to understand the Soviet experience in terms of the Jewish experience in the United States, and will regard them as roughly analogous. There can be no denying that the process of linguistic, cultural and religious falling away and assimilation has made deep inroads in American Jewry. Why can not the same process have been expected to produce similar results in the Soviet Union—accelerated, perhaps, by the nature of official policies?

Even without an exhaustive analysis of the analogy, it is easy to demonstrate how and why it can not hold up. To begin with, if we but compare the state of religious and cultural life in the two communities in, say, the year of the Revolution, there can be no question that Russian Jewry reveals itself as vastly richer and deeper, much more vibrant and vital and innovative—and could therefore, in the normal course of events and despite assimilation and falling off, have been expected to be at least as long-lived and even more vigorous and creative than American Jewry.

The essential difference between the two communities flows from the fundamental difference between an open and a closed society. In the one, options of all sorts are open to people. In the other, they are foreclosed. In America, Jews have enjoyed two basic kinds of options: they have been able to choose whether or not to remain Jews; and if to remain, in what ways to do so. In the USSR, Jews have not had such choices. Had they been available, there can hardly be any doubt how Jews would have chosen. The massive and passionate response of Soviet Jews of all ages to the single pathetic remnant of Jewish artistic expression—performances by wandering singers and actors of Yiddish songs and literary readings—is a case in point.

A telltale instance should suffice to underscore the point. When one considers the proliferation of thousands of Jewish schools and educational institutions and facilities, religious and secular, from elementary to post-graduate, in America, and when one considers that Soviet law permits any ten parents to arrange for educational classes for their children in their native language—it is astounding that there does not exist a single Jewish school or class for a community of more than three million, with its unique history and cultural background. It simply does not stand to reason that there should not be a group of ten Jewish parents who would want some education for their children in Jewish history, language and culture. It can only be fear and apprehension that keep them from requesting what they are legally entitled to.

There can be no denying that the combination of "natural" and "unnatural" processes in the USSR have taken a very heavy toll in terms of Jewish knowledge and cultural creativity. But it is readily demonstrable that Jewish national consciousness and the sense of Jewish identity, far from being moribund, are very much alive, strong and growing.

One elementary, indisputable fact, essential for an understanding of Soviet life, establishes at least the minimal groundwork for this analysis: No Soviet Jew can escape *identification* as a Jew simply because, like all Soviet citizens, his nationality is one of the vital statistics indicated in his internal passport. In a country where one's nationality is a key element in the very definition of one's citizenship, and where anti-Jewish discrimination and propaganda are ordinary facts of life, that identification, neutral or negative in itself, may nevertheless provide the basis for the transition to positive *identity*. The Soviet Jew may not even wish to fill that empty identification with content. He may not, even if he wishes to, know how to achieve meaningful identity. But he cannot escape the tag. He cannot avoid knowing that he is a Jew.

A word is in order about the definition of the phrase "Jewish national consciousness": Who can say what is a Jew? I shall attempt no definition when others, far more expert, have failed to reach agreement or even consensus. It is sufficient, in the present context, to begin by going along with the identification of the Soviet Jew in his passport. For lack of a better word, I use the word "national" in the broadest possible sense, including religious faith and affiliation, which may refer to any form of group identity. Finally, I use the word "consciousness" in an equally inclusive way, ranging over the entire spectrum of Jewish self-awareness—from those for whom such awareness is limited to their resentment of the discrimination they face, all the way over to those who demonstratively repudiate their Soviet citizenship and, *as Jews,* declare themselves citizens of the Jewish State of Israel and demand the right to go there.

Who are the Jews whose national consciousness is being probed?

Let me take the reader on a cultural-geographical *tour d'horizon* of the Jewish communities of the Soviet Union. For analytic purposes, I am dividing the map of the USSR into two main sections. One could be called the Soviet Heartland, the Slavic Heartland: Russia itself (RSFSR—Russian Soviet Federated Socialist Republic); the Ukraine; and Bielorussia. These three great republics constitute the overwhelming bulk of Soviet territory. On them, also, the vast majority of Soviet citizenry—and of Soviet Jewry—lives.

The second section is comprised of what may be called the Peripheral Territories. They are peripheral in several respects. To begin with, they are peripheral in the actual physical sense that they describe a huge semi-circle around the Slavic Heartland. Secondly, they are for the most part inhabited by non-Slavic peoples. Thirdly, they are also peripheral in the sense that some of them, at least, have not been parts of the Soviet Union for the full length of Soviet rule but were only absorbed at later dates, some as recently as the final phases of World War II.

It is helpful and illuminating to know how many Jews live in both the Soviet Heartland and the Peripheral Territories, for that figure gives us a clear idea of the size and extent of the population whose national consciousness we are attempting to gauge. A word of clarification is required at this point about the reliability of Soviet statistics on the Jews. A new Soviet census is to be taken in 1970 and it may well take a year and more before the results are published. All we can go on are the results of the last census, of 1959, and rule-of-thumb estimates.

The 1959 census provided the figure of 2,267,000 Jews. Yet most students of the subject have been using the estimate of 3,000,000. How is this discrepancy to be accounted for?

Although Soviet statistics are definitely more reliable now than in the past, they are still in many respects grossly inadequate and incomplete, and, like most things in the USSR, they are notoriously manipulable for political purposes. In the past decade, many knowledgeable, sophisticated Westerners have made innumerable contacts with Soviet Jews, who have consistently informed them that the figures on the Jews lie. The experience was reiterated in town after town: *They* say there are 10,000 Jews here, but *we* know from daily living that there are twice as many. It would certainly suit Soviet purposes to minimize the number of Jews as a means of intimating that there are fewer Jews than expected, so their problem is minimal.

Scores of thousands of Jews very likely did not cite themselves as such in the census, for they were not required to provide documentary evidence of their assertions of nationality. There must have been many Jews who wished, for whatever reasons, to conceal their identity to the extent possible, and felt they could get away with it in this instance.

[17]

Table I. THE BALTIC COUNTRIES

COUNTRY *Major City*	1959 Census Figures		Estimated Jewish Population	
LATVIA	36,592		40,000	
Riga		*30,267*		*35,000*
LITHUANIA	24,672		35,000	
Vilna		*16,354*		*25,000*
Kovno		*4,792*		*8,000*
ESTONIA	5,436		8,000	
Tallin		*3,714*		*5,000*
AREA TOTALS	66,700		83,000	

Table II. THE WESTERN REACHES OF EUROPEAN USSR

COUNTRY *Major City*	1959 Census Figures		Estimated Jewish Population	
WESTERN BIELORUSSIA	9,757		15,000	
Brest		*6,012*		
Grodno		*3,745*		
WESTERN UKRAINE	84,339		100,000	
Lvov Region		*30,030*		*35,000*
Bukovina (Chernovitz)		*42,140*		*50,000*
Transcarpathia		*12,169*		*15,000*
MOLDAVIA ⸜	95,107		130,000	
Kishinev		*42,934*		*65,000*
AREA TOTALS	189,203		245,000	

Table III. TRANS-CAUCASIA

COUNTRY *Major City*	1959 Census Figures		Estimated Jewish Population
GEORGIA	51,582		110,000
Tbilisi		*17,311*	
AZERBAIJAN	40,204		100,000
Baku		*29,197*	
RSFSR	32,261		40,000
Dagestan ASSR		*21,427*	
Chechen-Ingush ASSR		*5,223*	
Kabardino-Balkar ASSR		*3,529*	
N. Osetian ASSR		*2,082*	
AREA TOTALS	124,047		250,000

But recently, Soviet sources have tacitly repudiated their own census statistics and have begun to speak of three million Jews. If they are ready to admit that many, there must be many more.

The accompanying charts supply both the census figures and the informed estimates, which, incidentally, also take account of the natural increase in the course of a decade.

WE begin our cultural-geographical tour with the Peripheral Territories, among which several sub-categories are to be distinguished. They are:

1. *The Baltic Countries.* Latvia, Lithuania, Estonia.

2. *The Western Reaches of European USSR.* Western Bielorussia, Western Ukraine, Moldavia—all territories annexed after World War II.

3. *Trans-Caucasia.* Georgia, Azerbaijan, and the Caucasian segments of the RSFSR.

4. *Central Asia.* Uzbekistan, Kazakhstan, Tadjikistan, Kirghizia, Turkmenistan and the Siberian segments of the RSFSR.

Let us begin with a closer look at the first two groupings—the Baltic Countries and the Western Reaches of European USSR. These areas are more familiar to us for several reasons. They are among the most recent territorial acquisitions of the Soviet Union, having been annexed as a result of the War. But until about twenty-five years ago they were part of Europe: the Baltic lands had been independent, western Ukraine and western Bielorussia had been, essentially, eastern Poland, and Moldavia had been a part of Rumania. This vast slice of territory was also one of the main sources of East European Jewish immigration to the West in the late 19th and early 20th centuries, and is therefore more familiar territory to the immigrants' progeny.

One has only, if one knows something about East European Jewish cultural history, to call the roll of some of the main cities in that territorial belt to understand the richly creative role it played in Jewish religious, cultural and communal life: Riga, Dvinsk, Tels, Vilna, Kovno, Grodno, Baranovich, Pinsk, Brest, Rovno, Lvov, Munkach, Chernovitz, Kishinev. Today this area can still be described as an integral Jewish community. That community of approximately 350,000 has a direct, intense and still powerful bond to the Jewish life that thrived there before the War.

These were great cities of both traditional and modern Jewish learning, scholarship and education; cities bustling with Orthodox yeshivas and with secular Yiddish and Hebrew schools; cities where the whole panoply of Zionism, of the Jewish labor movement, of

Table IV. CENTRAL ASIA

COUNTRY *Major City*	1959 Census Figures		Estimated Jewish Population
UZBEKISTAN	94,344		130,000
Tashkent		50,445	
KAZAKHSTAN	28,048		40,000
Alma Ata		8,425	
TADJIKISTAN	12,415		18,000
Dushanbe		8,720	
KIRGHIZIA	8,610		10,000
Frunze		5,840	
TURKMENISTAN	4,078		5,000
Ashkhabad		1,276	
RSFSR	17,827		20,000
Tatar ASSR		10,360	
Bashkir ASSR		7,467	
AREA TOTALS	165,322		223,000

Table V. THE SOVIET HEARTLAND

COUNTRY *Major City*	1959 Census Figures		Estimated Jewish Population	
RSFSR	875,307		1,100,000	
Moscow		239,246		500,000
Leningrad		168,641		300,000
UKRAINE	840,311		1,000,000	
Kiev		153,466		225,000
BIELORUSSIA	150,084		250,000	
Minsk		38,842		
AREA TOTALS	1,865,702		2,350,000	

Yiddish and Hebrew literature and publications, was gloriously spread out. Most of the Jews were slaughtered and the community and its culture wiped out by the Nazis, and the Soviets never allowed any cultural reconstruction. But the suvivors of the Holocaust are the products of that past.

Virtually every Jew there possesses a Jewish education, or a profound and proud memory of Jewish learning and culture, and of

Jewish group kinship and national feeling. This striking phenomenon has been encountered by every Western visitor with any knowledge of Jewish history and any sense of Soviet reality.

Moving down to the bottom of the great semi-circle, we come to
Trans-Caucasia, where about a quarter of a million Jews live, including
a colorful community of Mountain Jews in the Dagestan ASSR, with a
Jewish language of their own called Tat. This is a community of
Oriental Jews, exotic and unfamiliar. (They are not to be designated,
as some mistakenly do, as Sephardic Jews; though these two groups
share certain common religious traditions, they are quite separate
entities, the Sephardim being descendants of the Jews of Spain who
were exiled in 1492, and the Oriental Jews possessing quite different
ancestry.) They do not have the Yiddish language, for example, which
is a common heritage of East European Jews, and their entire heritage
and socio-cultural outlook are radically disparate from the East
European tradition.

The Oriental Jews of Trans-Caucasia trace their ancestry directly
to the ancient land of Israel, perhaps from the time of the Roman
destruction of the Temple in Jerusalem (70 A.D.), and some claim
even farther back to Jews who left ancient Judea after the destruction
of Jerusalem by the Babylonians in 586 B.C. Obviously, their origins
are shrouded in myth and legend, but they have been living there as
long as anyone knows.

The Oriental Jews of the Caucauses are, like their non-Jewish
neighbors, vintners, shepherds, living an agrarian life totally un-
related to that of the East European Jews I have been describing.
Alongside the language of the area, they also usually have their own
Jewish language or dialect. Again like their neighbors, they are
bound together as distinctive entities by two traditionalistic and conservative (in the sense of "conserving") social institutions — religion
and the family. The family, the clan, are still potent elements in their
society, strengthening that traditionalism which in turn bolsters the
role of religion. Thus, it is not surprising to find that Orthodox
Judaism still retains a powerful hold on them to this day.

Anyone who has visited Georgia, for example, can testify to the
pervasive character of religion and religious institutions for most of
the people — and thus also, not surprisingly, for the Jewish minority.
It is important to note that for the Christians, who predominate
there, the Georgian Orthodox Church has always played a decisive
role in providing character and substance to Georgian national
sentiment, in being for centuries the only "national" institution that
perpetuated national traditions and hopes for national independence. This has unquestionably worked itself out into the evident
national pride and spirit of independence revealed by all Georgians,

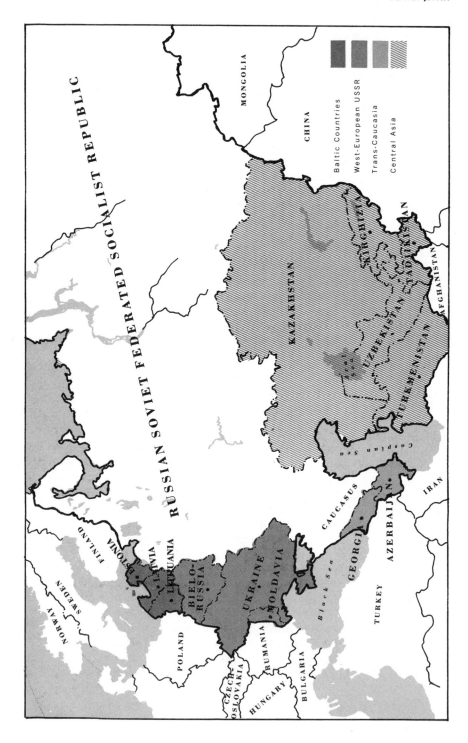

Baltic Countries

West-European USSR

Trans-Caucasia

Central Asia

MONGOLIA

CHINA

RUSSIAN SOVIET FEDERATED SOCIALIST REPUBLIC

KAZAKHSTAN

KIRGHIZIA

UZBEKISTAN

TADZHIKISTAN

TURKMENISTAN

AFGHANISTAN

Caspian Sea

CAUCASUS

IRAN

AZERBAIJAN

GEORGIA

TURKEY

Black Sea

ESTONIA

LATVIA

LITHUANIA

FINLAND

SWEDEN

NORWAY

BIELO-RUSSIA

UKRAINE

MOLDAVIA

POLAND

CZECHOSLOVAKIA

HUNGARY

RUMANIA

BULGARIA

and in the staunch support they give, even when they are secularized, to their national church. Something of this spirit of pride and
independence seems to have instilled itself also in the Jews of Georgia and the Caucauses, though not in so secularized a form.

(As is evident from this example, the attribution of strong Jewish
national consciousness to these Jews has little or nothing to do with
secular political matters, nor even only with ethnic feeling. In the
case of the Jews of Trans-Caucasia, it is their religion, along with
the family-clan, that binds them together as a recognizable, self-
aware, self-perpetuating group. But the non-secular character of the
binder does not make it any the less strongly national, in the flexible
sense I have been using.)

An excellent illustration is provided by their sense of the State
of Israel. There is no doubt of their profound attachment to it, but
in ways quite different from the East European Jews, whose feeling
for Israel is Western, modern, secular (though, of course, also molded,
ineluctably, by the force of age-old religious factors). The Jews of
Trans-Caucasia see Israel still as the ancient Holy Land, and they
think of their relationship with it, and with the Jewish people as a
whole, not in modern secular terms, but in Messianic religious
terms. For them, the Land of Israel is the Biblical land of their origins
— and their ultimate destiny is to return there in Messianic ways, if
not in Messianic days.

Now we move around eastward and northward from the Caucauses to the last great half of the huge semi-circle, to Central Asia.
The Uzbeks, Kazakhs, Kirghiz, Turkmens and Tadjiks who predominate here are of Turkic and Mongol origins, obviously non-Slavs—
and Moslem by religion. More quiescent and dispersed, less integrated nationally, than, say the Georgians, the conserving elements
of religion and clan also continue to play key roles in their lives.
And the same can be said for most of the Jews who live among them.
Like the Jews of Trans-Caucasia, they are Oriental Jews. But they
were even farther removed, geographically, from sources of viable
Jewish cultural and social life; and perhaps also because the non-
Jewish majority is less integrated nationally than the Georgians, the
Jews among them had become, by the turn of the century, quite iso-
lated, cut off and culturally moribund.

The situation began to change then, as the culturally renascent
Zionist movement of Russia started sending emissaries there to
revive Jewish leaning and national consciousness among the Oriental Jews. Modern Hebrew schools were established and the Jews
of Central Asia began to be revived and to be brought increasingly
back into the fold of the Jewish people. Though this trend was halted
in midstream by the Revolution, it was given a powerful impulse in

a more indirect way during World War II, when scores of thousands of Jews from Poland, the Baltic countries and the western reaches of the USSR made their way eastward to escape the Nazi hordes. Thus, in major cities like Tashkent, Alma Ata, Frunze and Dushanbe, new Jewish communities were created, some of which still persist today, and inevitably brought to bear upon the native Oriental Jews the impact of their strong Jewish national feelings. In this part of the semi-circle of peripheral territories, there live at least 165,000 Jews, by official count, and more like 225,000 in reality.

Altogether, then, the Peripheral Territories possess a Jewish population—however varied and disparate the separate communities may be in social structure, secularization, religion and culture—of from more than half a million (by the 1959 census) to more than three quarters of a million, by modest estimate. And these are all communities, regardless of their great differences, characterized by a profound and potent sense of Jewishness and of national consciousness.

WE arrive now, in our cultural-geographical *tour d'horizon*, to the Soviet Heartland—the RSFSR, Bielorussia, the Ukraine—where most Soviet citizens and the bulk of Soviet Jewry —anywhere from 1,865,000 to 2,350,000—live. It is here that the process of assimilation has gone much farther and penetrated much more deeply than elsewhere: Jews here have lived under the Communist regime twice as long as those in the major portions of the Peripheral Territories. Nevertheless, alongside the profundity of ignorance of things Jewish, there exists an extraordinary Jewish self-awareness, especially among those where it is least to be expected —the young generation.

In Moscow, in Leningrad, in Kiev and Odessa, in all the great cities of the Soviet Heartland, one encounters them, in the universities, on the streets, in the parks and restaurants, in the synagogues, at the seaside vacation resorts of the Baltic and Black Seas. Jews of all ages, not least the youth, eager to maintain or to rescuscitate some sort of Jewish connection or association, either with the Jewish past or with Jewish contemporaneity. They display great curiosity about Jewish life in other countries—but above all about the State of Israel. Even in an attenuated and dessicated way, the sense of the unity of the Jewish people remains largely intact, and it is symbolized and made concrete today for Soviet Jews—as for most Jews throughout the world—by the binding force of the State of Israel, its historical, religious, cultural, sentimental, familial connotations, and the reservoir of pride and national resurgence which it represents. Every sophisticated Western visitor who has made contact with Soviet Jews can testify to this.

The enormous significance of this factor — the undiminished force of the sense of unity of the Jewish people, regardless of its sources and the forms it assumes — cannot be over-emphasized. There is good historical reason — many good reasons, in fact — why this should be so. And just as I led you on a cultural-geographical *tour d'horizon* for the purpose of revealing the socio-cultural roots of the pervasive and persistent Jewish national consciousness, so now I would like to take you on a journey to survey the great and traumatic historical events and processes of the last quarter century that have had the effect of deepening and reinforcing that consciousness, that sense of Jewish unity.

As throughout Jewish history, it has been for Soviet Jews a unity in horror and despair as well as in joy and pride.

We must begin with the Nazi Holocaust, its impact, implications and consequences. To gain some slight insight into what the Holocaust meant to Soviet Jews, we have only to hark back to the mid-War years when the incredible tales of horror first began to emerge from the ghettoes and death camps. That whole still-inexplicable epoch unquestionably heightened Jewish self-awareness and group identity throughout the Western world, where the ghastly trauma was experienced only at second hand. Imagine, then, the impact upon Jews who actually bore the brunt of it, for we must not forget that the Germans conquered all the western reaches and penetrated deeply into the Soviet heartland. The great pioneer scholar of Soviet Jewish life, Solomon M. Schwarz, has estimated that as many as one million Jews were slaughtered by the Nazis on what is now Soviet territory. Aside from the Caucauses and Central Asia, there can hardly be a Jewish family in the USSR that did not lose a relative or a friend.

Now, for a particularly poignant insight, imagine, for example, the mood of the returning Soviet Jewish soldier at war's end. Though vastly outnumbered by the one hundred or so million Russians and Ukrainians, the tiny Jewish community supplied the third largest number, after those two others, of decorated war heroes of the Red Army. Already in the army the Jewish soldier encountered discrimination and humiliation. Upon his return, wounded perhaps, he further encounters two shocking phenomena: the diminution of the Jewish community in his home town and the overt anti-Semitism of his non-Jewish neighbors, undoubtedly exacerbated by the poisonous propaganda of the German occupiers. The burden of grief and sorrow, of bitterness and frustration, was surely potent and long-lasting. The deeply engraved lesson of the Holocaust was the historical continuum and shared experience of bestiality perpetrated upon Jews *qua* Jews.

The sense of unity and kinship was further bolstered just a few years later by another historic event, perhaps not less traumatic to the Jewish historical consciousness (or unconscious), but this time of a positive nature—the creation of the State of Israel in 1948. Once again, it is possible to ascertain that this event had the same kind of joyously overwhelming impact on Soviet Jews as on the Jews of the West. This time one need not imagine the impact: one has recourse to the moving eye-witness accounts of the appearance in Moscow of Israel's first ambassador, now Premier, Golda Meir. The picture of the throng of thousands of Jews following her on the Sabbath as she walked from the synagogue to her hotel: dancing, shouting, singing, touching, crying, men, women and children, a sight truly never to be forgotten.

THE pendulum swings again, from joy to sorrow, from Israel's creation to the Black Years. Those last five years of Stalin's life, characterized by the anti-Semitic, anti-cosmopolitan propaganda campaign and purge; the destruction of the remaining Jewish cultural institutions and the arrest, imprisonment and/or murder of the entire Jewish intelligentsia; the anti-Semitic trials and purges, á la Slansky, in several of the satellites; the Doctors' Plot. How could those dire, dark events not have pressed Jews back in on themselves, on a sharp consciousness of being Jews, unwanted aliens and second-class citizens.

Several years later, a much more subtle process began which would have made its own quiet contribution to bolstering Jewish national consciousness in the Soviet Union. In February 1956, the former leader, Nikita Khrushchev, made his famous "secret speech" unmasking Stalin as a monstrous criminal. It was the beginning of the policy of de-Stalinization which raised high hopes among most segments of Soviet society, especially the intelligentsia, that the process would be far-reaching and would move the country along a more decent and humane path. And certainly the Jews must also have expected that if things would ease up in general Soviet life, conditions would become easier for the Jews as well. And so hopes were raised . . . and then they were dashed—because nothing of the sort happened, least of all for the Jews. The dashing of these hopes, the plunge back into quiet frustration and desperate resignation, would have made its own kind of subtle contribution to bolstering Jewish identity.

Not only did things not ease up for the Jews, they worsened, especially in the first five years of the 1960s. Those years witnessed two massive nationwide phenomena, naturally directed from the center, that had the most deleterious socio-psychological consequences for the Jews. The first of these was the renewal of a vigorous propaganda drive aimed at eradicating still potent residues of religious faith. This campaign addressed itself to all religions, of course. But in Soviet circumstances, it is virtually inevitable that an anti-religious propaganda campaign directed at Judaism and conducted with the typical virulence and crudity of Soviet polemics should devolve into a wholesale expression of anti-Semitism.

So, in a country where anti-Semitism has an ancient, one might almost say honorable, tradition, and where it is still pervasive and endemic, it becomes easy and natural for the anti-religious propagandist aiming at Judaism to fall back spontaneously on traditional, readily understood and acceptable, anti-Semitic stereotypes. Thus Abraham is attacked not merely as the first believer in the false doctrine of religious monotheism, but as a fellow who cheated his non-Jewish neighbors. Joshua is reviled as the first imperialist conqueror of ancient Palestine, a precursor of modern-day Zionist imperialism. Or, it's not just that King David lusted after other men's wives (that's only to be expected from the author of the religious Psalms), but that he was, characteristically, leader of a Jewish state that pursued aggressive ambitions. The ancient Israelites are portrayed in the same colors as the synagogue Jews of today—superstitious, money-mad, thieving connivers. And the Bible is the Book of *that* People . . .

During the same period, 1961-64, a great campaign was conducted all over the country against so-called economic crimes, chiefly embezzlement of state funds and property, giving and taking bribes, dealing in foreign currency, and currency speculation. Now in the Soviet Union almost everybody steals something, and bribery is a comparatively common phenomenon. Apparently the situation became so bad in the late 1950s that by 1960-61 a decision was made to try to eradicate as much of this crime as possible. Into this massive campaign were thrown all the means and know-how at the disposal of the authorities—including the death penalty, which was revived for the purpose. All the major newspapers and communications media, the party apparatus, the volunteer militia, the secret police, and the ordinary institutions of government were mobilized for this campaign. A virulent propaganda drive ensued. Moreover, the courts were brought into play and mass trials took place involving many thousands of accused. Much of the propaganda, indeed, focused on these court cases—beginning with the arrest and preliminary investigation of the alleged culprits, going through their arraignments and trials, and finally their sentences.

In this enormous three-and-a-half-year campaign, the Jews were the scapegoats and prime victims. The vituperative hate campaign exploited all the old anti-Semitic stereotypes involving the Jew's relation to money. Most of the more egregious trials featured Jewish

[27]

culprits. Tens of thousands of people, if not many more, were involved, but it was the Jews on whom the attention concentrated. And of the approximately 250 people sentenced to death, 50-55 per cent were Jews; in the Ukraine, where popular anti-Semitism was rife, the proportion reached higher than 80 per cent.

The effect of this double-barreled campaign, against religion and economic offenses, can only be imagined, not only concerning the Jewish victims, but for all Jews who had only to read the vicious stereotypes to recognize that, however innocent, all Jews were somehow inculpated.

And alongside the specific high and low points, traumatic events and hostile policies, throughout the long years of the '40s, '50s and '60s, the Jews have had to live with the knowledge of pervasive discrimination against them in the streets, in seeking higher education and in obtaining employment. Though this kind of thing is impossible to document, everyone in the USSR, Jew and non-Jew, knows that it is harder for Jewish students to gain admission to the universities, and they have to compile better records, once in, to stay in; everyone knows that there are some areas, "security sensitive" areas, from which Jews are entirely or virtually excluded — government and party leadership positions, the foreign service, the foreign trade and cultural exchange apparatus, military leadership, military-related science; everyone knows that even in those areas where Jews are free to enter and even to rise, they cannot rise to the highest levels to which their native gifts would normally lead them (except for a handful of undeniable geniuses).

The impact of all of this was beautifully illustrated by the late Maurice Hindus, a keen, life-long observer of Soviet society, in a characteristic and telling little incident he recounted in his 1961 book, *House Without A Roof.* An assimilated Soviet Jewish intellectual told him of the shattering experience of his ten-year-old son who came home from school one day crying, having been beaten up by Russian school-mates. They yelled that he and his kind were not wanted at the school, and they should all go back to Israel, where all Jews belong.

"The strange part of it is," said the father, "that the boy had never before even heard of Israel, and now he wants to know all about it."

ONCE again, Israel — the palpable symbol of Jewish unity and continuity. The final and most recent historic event to cite is the Soviet Jewish response to the rise of the Middle East crisis in May 1967, and especially to the Six-Day War and the famous Israeli victory that June. There is an enormous amount of evidence testifying to the fact that Soviet Jews reacted to the crisis, the war and the victory precisely as did the Jews of the West. It was one of the moral and emotional high points of their lives, and by itself contributed powerfully to the strengthening and deepening of a vibrant Jewish national consciousness in the Soviet Union. It is even possible to speculate that this most intoxicating event led a segment of Soviet Jewish youth to break out of the more accepted forms of relatively muted expressions of Jewish identity, and to break through to a radically new form of national self-assertion.

It is possible to point, over the past twenty years or so, to a gradual expansion of national feeling, to a fascinating spiritual transformation of a sizable segment of Soviet Jewish youth, to a point where today many young Jews — university students, professionals, even Komsomol members — say openly: "I do not go to the synagogue; I do not believe in Judaism as a religion. But I am a Jew and want to be known as a Jew."

Marks and manifestations of Jewish national feeling and consciousness have been in manifold evidence for at least two decades. One might begin in 1947, with the announcement of plans by Jewish cultural leaders for the renewal of Jewish book and periodical publication on a large scale and for the rebirth of other Jewish cultural institutions in the Yiddish language. Or one could begin in 1948, with the fabled procession of Golda Meir and her Soviet Jewish mass entourage. One could cite the massive Jewish attendance, in the hundreds of thousands and the cumulative millions, at the periodic performances of Yiddish music and literary readings since 1955, when they were first permitted. Or the great popularity of the amateur Yiddish theatre troupes of Vilna and Kishinev. Of great revelatory significance are the 1959 census figures on Yiddish as a mother tongue. Fully 20 per cent of the Jews listed Yiddish as their mother tongue — which is quite remarkable, considering the depradations made upon Jewish culture and Yiddish in the preceding decades. Even more interesting, in this connection, is the fact that 50 per cent listed Yiddish as their mother tongue in Moldavia and Latvia — and 70 per cent in Lithuania (tell-tale signs of Jewish national consciousness and identity in the Peripheral Territories).

One could go on endlessly with anecdotes that tell the identical story. The tremendous applause that Jewish ditties get when played by orchestras in Moscow restaurants. The encounters with families at seaside summer resorts, at the beaches, where youngsters will identify themselves as Jewish and eagerly ask for some trinket — a coin, an amulet, a sexagonal Star of David that historically identifies the Jew, a necklace — from Israel.

Or the Jewish *Samizdat*. Samizdat is a Soviet Russian neologism that translates roughly as "Your Own Publishing Company," as distinguished from the official. Samizdat refers to the vast amount of underground literature that circulates in manuscript form from hand to hand, whether it is a novel by Solzhenitsyn or a poem by some unknown fledgeling. There is a Jewish Samizdat also—manuscripts of Jewish substance in Yiddish, Hebrew and Russian, circulating in this great country. There is still another kind of Jewish Samizdat: tapes of Yiddish and Hebrew songs taken from Radio Israel (to which *all* listen devoutly) and passing from hand to hand by young people especially.

There were the tumultuous scenes of applause and welcome for Geulah Gill, an Israeli folk singer who was mobbed by cheering crowds of youngsters at her appearances, especially in Riga in 1966. And then there was the stunning experience of Israel's Deputy Premier Yigal Allon in the spring of 1967, not long before the outbreak of the Israel-Arab War. Then Labor Minister, he had come to Moscow as a member of the Israeli delegation to an international conference on social security. Allon, it should be remembered, was commander of the Palmach, the striking force of the Haganah, the Jewish army of Palestine that fought through to Israel's independence in 1948—and the Palmach had a powerful marching song that subsequently became a hit in Israel. At a reception for him at the Israel Embassy, Allon found himself suddenly surrounded by dozens of Moscow Jewish students and young people who had materialized from nowhere—and who sang his rousing old 1948 song for him! How did they know he was coming to the USSR? How did they discover he would be at a reception at the Embassy that night? Where did they learn that song?

One can point to the large-scale circulation, in manuscript, of Leon Uris' emotional Zionist novel *Exodus* in Russian translation (its official publication is, naturally, prohibited). And to the subterranean distribution of the tape, recorded from Israel's short-wave radio, of the Hebrew song that became the anthem of Israel's 1967 victory—*Yerushalayim shel Zahav (Jerusalem the Golden)*.

TIME was that fear dominated the hearts of Soviet Jews, and those who guarded the flame did so in secret and stealth. The fear is still there, of course, especially among the elderly, but a new generation is arising, of young people who yearn for knowledge and pride as Jews.

By far the best known and strikingly dramatic illustration of this new phenomenon is the open demonstrativeness, even defiance, that has been manifested by growing numbers of Jewish youngsters in recent years. It began about five years ago,[1] when about one hundred students gathered in the courtyard of the main Moscow synagogue on the eve of *Simchat Torah*, the autumn festival that celebrates the conclusion of the annual cycle of Pentateuch reading. Since then, their numbers have grown by leaps and bounds, so that in the last couple of years scores of thousands have gathered in front of the synagogues, not just in Moscow but in Leningrad and other cities, to sing and dance Yiddish and Hebrew songs and dances all the night through. They come not to pray, not to hear the Torah chant, but to identify openly and proudly as Jews.

I don't know of a single authority on Soviet affairs, or of a single expert on Soviet Jewish life, who predicted this phenomenon, or even had the slightest inkling of it in advance. What, then, has happened to the logic of history here? How did it happen that tens of thousands of youngsters, who know nothing Jewish, not a Jewish word in Hebrew or Yiddish, nothing of Jewish history—how did it happen that they, of all people, should arrive at a new sense of pride and consciousness? I have tried to explain it historically and using social scientific analysis. But in the end it remains, perhaps, a mystery.

Of this, however, there can be little doubt—that a vast number of Soviet Jews would choose, in one form or another, to exercise their natural right to group life, to act upon the basic human right of a historic people to perpetuate its group existence, to implement the right of individuals to find self-realization through their natural kinship with their people.

For many, this would simply mean the chance to perform their religious duties and to maintain religious associations without administrative hindrance. For many more, this would mean at least the opening of social-cultural clubs and centers where Jewish young people might foregather. For many others, this would mean the opportunity to establish—with the kind of support and encouragement which the regime gives all other nationalities—cultural, educational, artistic and communal institutions that would assure to succeeding generations a knowledge of Jewish history, culture and literature. And, finally, for those who can find self-realization only in their ancient homeland, this would mean the right to leave the USSR in order to create a new Jewish life for themselves in Israel.

(It is remarkable, in this connection, that the most recent appeal for human rights and civil liberties, issued in June 1969 by fifty-four courageous Soviet intellectuals, protested trials of Jews seeking to exercise their right to emigrate to Israel!)

Striking testimony to the readiness of many Soviet Jews to adopt the latter option appears in the documents appended to this study —the memorandum of the Lithuanian intellectuals, the letter by the young engineer Kochubiyevsky, and the letter from three Moscow Jews. (The other document—a proposal to create a Jewish theatre— testifies, of course, to the desire of many Jews for their own cultural

institutions; though it pays the required lip-service to official ideological rhetoric, its intention is unmistakable.) Let us go, they cry.
We want to live as Jews in the land of the Jews!

The Jews of the USSR have an especial claim on the conscience of
mankind. That claim rests above all on the fact that they represent
the last remnant of the spiritually prolific East European community
that was wiped out by the Nazis. Those who survive deserve the
right to work out their destiny unmolested, with humanity's troubled
heart on guard for them . . . as it was not for the others.

[1] 1964

[*The following letter, whose authenticity is well-vouched for,
was sent February 1968 to the Central Committee of the Lithuanian Communist Party by twenty-six anonymous Jewish
residents of Vilna in protest against the rising tide of anti-
Semitism in Soviet Lithuania. It reached the Western world in
September through the agency of an American tourist.*]

AN APPEAL

To COMRADE A. SNIETSKUS, First Secretary of the Central Committee of the Lithuanian Communist Party

WE, COMMUNIST AND NON-PARTY REPRESENTATIVES of the Jewish intelligentsia who have discussed and signed this document, address ourselves
to the Central Committee of the Lithuanian Communist Party because of our
great anxiety about the rising wave of anti-Semitism in Soviet Lithuania. We
draw the attention of the Central Committee to the fact that the earth has not

yet grown cold in Ponar and in the Ninth Fort of Kaunas, the soil that had been watered with the blood of our parents, brothers and sisters;[1] we draw the attention of the Central Committee to the fact that at the sites of mass murder, where tens of thousands of Jews lie buried, no monuments have been built thus far similar to that in Piritsiupys, which was erected to commemorate one hundred innocently murdered Lithuanians; we draw the attention of the Central Committee to the fact that 25,000 Jews living in Soviet Lithuania have not forgotten who carried out the mass murders.[2]

We realize that the anti-Israel propaganda conducted by the Soviet press is not intended for internal consumption and is not directed at Jews who live in the Soviet Union. However, we should not ignore the fact that, despite all the stylistic nuances, this anti-Israel propaganda, and especially the cartoons in the central press, have revived anti-Semitic passions in a certain part of the Lithuanian (and not only the Lithuanian) people. Therefore, we can not be silent at a time when in the present tense situation new notes emerge that give a local character to the entire matter. We can not be silent when the press publishes material that nourishes local judeophobia.

The weekly newspaper *Kalba Vilnius (Vilnius Speaking*, No. 7, page 14) has published quotations depicting Jews as a traditional object of mockery, which ethnologist S. Skrodenis has painstakingly selected from the writings of Lithuanian classics. As one reads them, one gets the idea that mocking Jews is an old "tradition" of the Lithuanian people. The author Skrodenis knew what he was doing in his article, "Winter, Winter, Get Out Of The Yard." In the traditional Shrovetide processions, the personages of a drunken Russian bureaucrat and "honorable" Polish landed gentry figured next to Jews, gypsies and Germans [*among those mocked—ed.*], and sometimes even dominated the event. The cited writings of Zemaite, Jucevicius and Valancius are full of anti-Russian and anti-Polish statement. All one needs to do is to select them properly and present them together in one place.

However, the author Skrodenis and the editors of *Kalba Vilnius* know that it is not allowed to mock a drunken Russian bureaucrat or an "honorable" Polish landowner, while one can write about Jews *now*. Only in this way can one explain the painstaking ethnographic selection.

More than that. The editors of *Kalba Vilnius* express regret about the following: "Such processions of costumed people have almost completely disappeared today; and while somewhere deep in the Zamaitija region some still do it, they are a little afraid. This is because in some regions the keepers of public order simply forbid it." The newspaper urges the "revival of beautiful popular traditions." What is this—an open invitation to stage anti-Semitic manifestations, under the cover of reviving "popular traditions"?

On this occasion we would like to point out that, because of the one-sidedness of our propaganda, objective conditions have been created for the flourishing of anti-Semitism. Individual leading personalities, Communists, are quite openly promoting it and are personally willing to express it. Here are several facts out of many:

When the Deputy Minister of Trade, Kazbaras, was reproached for not observing the Leninist principle of selecting cadres on the basis of their political and technicial qualifications, he replied publicly: "To be a Lithuanian in Soviet Lithuania is a political qualification."

The Deputy Chairman of Television, Kuolelis, openly criticized a correspondent in a meeting for his Jewish mannerisms on the screen.

The President of the Pedagogical Institute, Uogintas, bluntly told one of the instructors: "It matters little that today you excel others in the German or English languages, in physics or mathematics, chemistry or music. We will develop our own cadres so that tomorrow Lithuanians will be more qualified than you." All Uogintas did was to give public expression to a principle that has been in force for a long time in cadre [employment] policy.

Here are the facts. During the entire postwar period, not a single Jewish student living in Lithuania (except for a few children of privileged persons) was given a state scholarship to continue his studies at institutions of higher learning in Moscow or Leningrad. Not a single Jew originating from Lithuania has taken post-graduate courses in the institutes of Moscow or Leningrad. Not a single Jewish Communist has attended the Academy of Social Sciences or the Party University of the Soviet Communist Party's Central Committee (except M. Bordonaite).

And here are the facts about the distribution of cadres. Ten percent of the inhabitants of Vilnius are Jews. Until now not a single Jew has ever been elected chairman, deputy chairman or secretary of the city or of the city's four regional executive committees. Since the dismissal of Atamukas, not a single Jewish Communist has ever been elected secretary of a Party city committee or a city-region committee, nor have any been appointed department heads by the corresponding plenums.

Not a single Jew has been elected judge of a people's court. Not a single Jew has been elected to any higher position in the trade unions. During the entire postwar era, not a single representative of Jewish youth has risen to a leading position in state, party or trade union activity—while at the same time the mass of Lithuanian cadres has been educated and promoted during the postwar years. In fact, only a handful of meritorious Jewish revolutionaries of the older generation are still merely tolerated in higher positions, and they are now being hurriedly pushed out to pension as soon as possible.

We know that the Jewish cultural institutions in Lithuania were destroyed not at the initiative of the Central Committee of the Lithuanian Communist Party, and therefore we do not think there is any need to raise this question now. Yet none of us have forgotten the summary punishment of Ceserkas — violinist, veteran Communist underground fighter, veteran of the Fatherland war—who had dared (as the Lithuanian clandestine teachers had done in 1863-1905, when 'the press was prohibited in Lithuania) to teach a group of young Jews the alphabet of their native tongue. He was dismissed from the Party and thrown out from everywhere.

As for the protection of Jewish cultural monuments, it must be stated that not a single synagogue structure that survived the Occupation has been declared an architectural monument under state protection, whereas a considerable number of Catholic churches and architectural monuments are protected by the state and repaired at its expense. Moreover, one of the most outstanding architectural monuments of 16th-century Lithuania, the underground synagogue of the Gaon of Vilna (at the intersection of Muziejus and Rudininkai Streets), was deliberately destroyed and desecrated during the doctors' trial in Moscow in 1952.

Local authorities, with obvious connivance or even silent consent from above, are destroying Jewish cemeteries, while the cattle of the townspeople graze on those that remain. Tombstones are used as building materials even for the construction of public buildings. Even the Hitlerites had left Jewish cemeteries untouched throughout the period of their occupation of Lithuania. The Jewish cemeteries of Sovietsk (formerly Tilsit) or Cherniavski (formerly Insterburg) in East Prussia remained untouched through all the thirteen years of Hitler's rule. Only now have they been completely destroyed without warning (even the foreign radio commented on this). Pink marble from the old Jewish cemetery in Vilnius was used for the pedestal of the Pushkin monument, erected at the foot of the Gediminas hill in Vilnius. This act of vandalism insults not only the Jews but everyone who respects Pushkin's genius.

We do not wish to over-state the case. By no means. We know that the situation of the Jews is considerably better in Lithuania than in other parts of the USSR; especially terrible is the discrimination against our compatriots in the Ukraine. During the entire postwar period in Lithuania there was only one bloody pogrom, in Plunge in 1958, while, according to our information, not fewer than twenty pogroms have occurred in the Ukraine. (Victims were especially numerous in Shachty, Gorlovka and other towns.)

We highly value the Lithuanian Communist Party, the traditional internationalism of its Central Committee, and the national tolerance of the Lithuanian people. Nevertheless, as the chairman of the state security committee, Petkevicius, stated at the plenum of the Lithuanian Communist Party's Central Committee—emigrational tendencies are increasing among the Jewish inhabitants. It is known that if the borders would be opened for emigration today, some eighty per cent of the entire Jewish populace would leave Soviet Lithuania and depart for Israel. These people would leave everything here—despite the unsettled conditions in the Near East, despite the fact that our people in this country are used to a damp climate and would find it difficult to acclimatize there, despite the fact that almost no one among Lithuanian Jews knows Hebrew anymore or observes religious traditions, despite the fact that their present qualifications (most economically active people are employed in service occupations) would not make it easy for them to become integrated into Israel's society.

We are confronted with a paradox here. We are not wanted here, we are being completely oppressed, forcibly denationalized, and even publicly insulted in the press—while at the same time we are forcibly kept here. As the Lithuanian proverb goes, "He beats and he screams at the same time."

We are not speaking to you about the noble Communist ideals, about the equality of men and nations, about proletarian internationalism. All these slogans have been thrown into the dust-heap of demagogy long ago. They have been replaced now by one slogan: "Love for the great Russian people, and what is left from that 'love' let us divide up among ourselves." The authors of this document are appealing only to your, and your colleagues' universal human, democratic convictions. Do all in your power to put down the menacingly rising wave of anti-Semitism. It is not too late yet. If that is not done now, Lithuania will again "adorn itself" with new Ponars and Ninth Forts.

It has been decided not to make public the surnames of the twenty-six signers of this document. We know well how people who had protested against flourishing anti-Semitism in the Soviet Union at one time or another were dealt with summarily. The

Party has taught us to be watchful, and we have to be watchful now as we write to the Central Committee of the Lithuanian Communist Party. What painful irony!

Vilnius, February 15, 1968

---

[1] Ponar is the site on the outskirts of Vilna, Lithuania's capital, where the Nazis massacred the tens of thousands of Jews of the city and its environs. The Ninth Fort was a military structure in a suburb of Kovno (Kaunas), Lithuania's second city, where a similar Jewish holocaust occurred. The signers of the petition refer here to the well-known Soviet policy of imposed silence about Jewish martyrdom under the Nazis, a psychological gambit in the attempt to eradicate Jewish consciousness from among Soviet Jews.

[2] In most cases, it was the Germans' Lithuanian henchmen who actually performed the mass executions, under Nazi supervision.

The Case of Boris L. Kochubiyevsky

Boris Lvovich Kochubiyevsky was born in Kiev, the Ukraine, in 1936. His father and grandparents were killed by the Nazis at Babi Yar, the charnel house on the outskirts of Kiev where tens of thousands of Jews were slaughtered in September 1941.

The boy was brought up in an orphanage and attended a trade school. Later, he received an engineering degree from the Kiev Polytechnical Institute. He had no Jewish education or culture and his wife, Larisa Aleksandrovna Kochubiyevsky, is non-Jewish. Still, his experiences as a Jew in the Soviet Union made him always aware of his Jewish origins.

In June 1967, at a meeting organized at his factory to protest "Israeli aggression," Kochubiyevsky heatedly rejected the official line and upheld Israel's right of defense. At a subsequent meeting of his factory trade union, his action was discussed and he was asked to resign, which he refused to do.

At a memorial meeting at Babi Yar in February 1968, Kochubiyevsky once more overtly contradicted an official Soviet line. This time he protested the Soviet policy of minimizing or even keeping silent about the Jewish massacre at Babi Yar.

In May 1968, he finally succumbed to pressure and resigned his job. That summer, he and his wife applied for exit permits to Israel; they were refused. But in November, they were given permission to leave and were told to appear at the passport office on November 28 to pick up their documents.

That morning, however, their apartment was searched and many of his letters were seized, among them protest letters written to Soviet authorities.

The following week, Kochubiyevsky was arrested. His wife, after refusing pressures to leave him and divorce him, was expelled from the Teachers College where she was a student, and from the Komsomol. His arrest was based on Article 187, Chapter 1, of the Ukrainian criminal code, and it cited his statements at the above-mentioned occasions.

On May 16, 1969, Kochubiyevsky was sentenced to three years in prison. His trial was conducted in a typically authoritarian as well as anti-Semitic way. His defense counsel was permitted only to agree with the essential charges of the prosecution. The courtroom was packed with people who voiced anti-Semitic sentiments and the judge did nothing to quell them.

In his final plea, Kochubiyevsky took note of this atmosphere and of the fact that the trial had taken place in the very same building and room where the Beilis blood libel trial of ·1911 had occurred. And he declared:

"In condemning me, you will only encourage anti-Semitism."

His open letter follows:

November 28, 1969

To: *The Secretary General of the CPSU Central Committee — Brezhnev; The First Secretary of the (Ukraine CP) Central Committee — Shelest*

Copy: *To the Investigator of the Prosecutor's Office of the Shevchenko Region of the City of Kiev — V. V. Doroshenko*

From: *The accused of slander against Soviet reality — B. L. Kochubiyevsky, Jew.*

I AM A JEW. I want to live in the Jewish State. This is my right, just as it is the right of a Ukrainian to live in the Ukraine, the right of a Russian to live in Russia, the right of a Georgian to live in Georgia.

I want to live in Israel.

This is my dream, this is the goal not only of my life but also of the lives of hundreds of generations preceding me that were expelled from the land of their ancestors.

I want my children to study in a school in Hebrew. I want to read Jewish papers. I want to go to a Jewish theatre. What's wrong with that? What is my crime? Most of my relatives were shot by the fascists. My father was killed and his parents were killed. Were they alive now, they would stand at my side: Let me go!

I have appealed with this request many times to various departments and I have achieved only this: Dismissal from my job; the expulsion of my wife from her institute; and, to top it all, a criminal charge of slandering Soviet reality. Of what does this slander consist? Is it slander that in the multi-national Soviet state only the Jewish people cannot teach its children in Jewish schools? Is it slander that in the USSR there are no Jewish papers? Incidentally, no one even denies this. Perhaps it is slander that for over a year I have not succeeded in obtaining an exit permit for Israel? Or is it slander that people don't want to speak to me, that there is no one to complain to? Nobody reacts. But even this isn't the heart of the matter. I don't want to be involved in the national affairs of a State in which I consider myself an outsider. I want to go away from here. I want to live in Israel. My wish does not contradict Soviet laws.

I have an invitation from relatives; all the formalities have been observed. Is that why you are instituting a criminal case against me?

Is that why my home was searched?

I am not asking for mercy. Listen to the voice of reason: Let me go!

As long as I live, as long as I am capable of feeling, I shall devote all my strength to obtain an exit permit for Israel. And even if you should find it possible to sentence me for it, I shall anyway, if I live long enough to be freed, be prepared even then to make my way even on foot to the homeland of my ancestors.

Kochubiyevsky

[*Following is another example of the resurgence of Jewish national consciousness in the USSR.*]

To the Chairman of the Council of Ministers of the U.S.S.R., A. N. KOSYGIN

From Citizens U. I. KLAIZMER, V. I. BORUKHOVICH and B. L. SHLEIN, *who live at the following address: Moscow Zh. 457*
Pervaya Novokuzminskaya #6, Apt. 72

OPEN LETTER

IN VIEW OF THE FACT that our many letters, statements and appeals to you personally, as well as to other highly placed Soviet statesmen, have met with no response, we have decided to turn with this letter to those press organs that will understand the tragedy of our situation and will agree to publish this letter.

We the undersigned constitute one family and are Jews by nationality. On December 30, 1968, basing ourselves upon the formal affidavit of invitation [*vizov, required by Soviet regulations — Translator*] from our sisters, we applied for exit permits to the State of Israel in order to be reunited with close relatives from whom we were separated as a result of the war and whom we have not seen for thirty years.

On June 16, 1969, our application was denied, our natural human urge to live with our closest relatives, with our people and in the land of our people was rejected.

We consider that fact that our request was under consideration for nearly six months only to be rejected, as an appalling act of mocking humiliation and anti-Semitism.

Our family was educated in the tradition of Jewish culture but in the present conditions of Soviet reality our children are denied the possibility of learning their own language, as well as the great cultural heritage and all the spiritual values of our people, because unlike other peoples living in the U.S.S.R. the Jewish people is subjected to cruel discrimination: There exist in the U.S.S.R. neither Jewish schools nor any other Jewish institutions of learning nor theatres, since the bloody repressions of 1948-1953; there exist no periodical Jewish publications except one lone magazine.

Absolutely everything connected with the achievements of the Jewish people's philosophers and men of culture, science and art, everything connected with the heroism of the Jewish people and the sufferings it experienced — everything Jewish, in short, is silenced.

Books by a writer like Kichko, informed with a consistent and open anti-Semitic spirit on the level of the propaganda of the Tsarist Black Hundreds, are published and popularized. All this profoundly insults our national feelings and our human dignity, and to remain in such an atmosphere of anti-Semitic propaganda and discrimination is unbearable to us.

We feel ourselves to be Jews emotionally and spiritually, bound up with our Jewish State of Israel. As free men who have committed no crimes, in full consonance with the Constitution of the U.S.S.R. as well as with the basic principles of the Convention on the Liquidation of All Forms of Racial Discrimination, and in accordance with the statement you made at a press conference in Paris in November [*actually December — Translator*] 1966, we have the full right of emigrating to Israel.

We would like to hope that you will reveal understanding and that our request will be complied with.

[*signed*]

KLAIZMER
BORUKHOVICH
SHLEIN

25, June, 1969

The attached memorandum, translated from Russian, was submitted many months ago by a large group of distinguished Jewish professional theatre people to the headquarters of the Soviet Community Party in Moscow. As can be seen, these Soviet Jewish artists plead for the establishment of a professional Jewish theatre in Kiev. The list of those backing the proposal, also expressing readiness to work in such a theatre, includes the well known Soviet Jewish composers, Pulver and Weinberg, as well as numerous playwrights, directors and others. Among them are the following theatre people, all of whom have been the recipients not only of critical praise but of official honors:

M. I. GOLDBLATT, *Honored Artist of the RSFSR (Russian Republic)*

I. KOLIN, *Honored Artist of the RSFSR*

YU. MINKOVS, *Honored Artist of the RSFSR*

V. SHVARTSER, *Honored Artist of the RSFSR*

I. TREPEL, *Honored Artist of the BSSR (Bielorussian Republic)*

J. ARONCHIK, *People's Artist of the BSSR*

M. SOKOL, *People's Artist of the BSSR*

Although this memorandum was presented a long time ago, it has not yet been graced with a reply from on high.

March 1967

THEATRE ART HAS PLAYED a prominent role in the spiritual life of the Jewish workers for a very long time, and continues to do so. In pre-revolutionary Russia there existed many theatrical groups which, despite harsh oppression, brought their living artistic message to the masses. And, as a rule, what they had to say was of a clearly democratic and progressive character.

After the Great October Socialist Revolution, when the Jews, along with all the peoples of our Homeland, gained the right to build their own culture — national in form and socialist in content — the Jewish theatre was reborn on new, Soviet principles. Young people drawn to the theatre gained admission to general institutions of learning for the theatre, and special national theatre groups also made their appearance. The professional Jewish theatre undertook a wide range of activities. It is sufficient to mention that until the Great Patriotic War there were about ten such theatres in the USSR, and they enjoyed State support and great success with their audiences.

During the War, in addition to the hundreds of thousands of Jewish soldiers who died the death of the brave on the battlefield, a huge number of civilians also perished — brutally murdered by the fascist invaders. This vast and unprecedented national catastrophe naturally also resulted in the shrinkage of the theatrical "market," and after the war the number of Jewish State Theatres decreased to three — in Moscow, Minsk and Chernovtsy. This was the situation until 1950.

At present there is not a single Jewish theatre in the entire Soviet Union, despite the fact that a considerable segment of the nearly three million Soviet Jews knows the Yiddish language and feels the need for its own national Soviet Theatre. This is why we are convinced that the establishment of a Jewish theatre is quite advisable now.

The basic task of this theatre would be to aid in educating the Jewish spectator in the spirit of Marxism-Leninism.

There is a considerable number of Jewish actors, now working in various theatres or in different aspects of theatre life, who are ready at any time to undertake the establishment of a Soviet Jewish theatre. Suffice it to note that in the Ukraine alone there are now more than sixty former actors of the Jewish stage, among whom are masters with great experience and titles of honor, as well as talented younger people.

The same may be said for playwrights who write in Yiddish and from whom can be expected the creation of original plays on modern Soviet themes, as well as the translation into Yiddish of the best works by Soviet playwrights and of the Russian and world classics.

As for the masses of Jewish workers, they await the creation of such a theatre with impatience. They evince great interest in any Yiddish variety show or concert performance, and it would be more than desirable, so as to obviate hackwork and unsupervised work, to create a single, party-controlled center of art culture in the Ukraine.

It is most unfortunate that the authorities in charge of the theatre do not display a sufficiently serious attitude toward this question; at best, they tend to be satisfied with the creation of two or three small itinerant theatrical troupes. At the same time, the creation of a central Jewish repertory theatre as a full-fledged State cultural institution would serve as a brilliant refutation of what our enemies abroad say about the suppression of Jewish national culture in the USSR.

In view of all this, we take the liberty of requesting that you hasten the resolution of the question of establishing a Jewish State repertory theatre in Kiev; it is now ripe for favorable action. This theatre would function in its own permanent locale in Kiev for five or six months out of the year, and would serve the towns of the Ukrainian SSR during the rest of the year.

In the Ukraine alone we have 25 centers with sufficiently large Jewish populations to supply audiences: In Odessa, Kharkov, Lvov, Dniepropetrovsk, Chernovtsy, Poltava, Belaya Tserkov, Khmelnitsky, Zhitomir, Chernigov, Krivoy Rog, Vinnitsa, Cherkassy, Ternopol, Kamenets-Podolsk.

Such a theatre — by adopting the correct repertory policy which takes into account the audience's heightened ideological and artistic demands — would be able, we are sure, not only to work without a State subsidy, but even to produce a clear profit. The main purpose of this theatre must be the education of the Jewish spectator in the spirit of Marxism-Leninism, the mobilization of the will, the feelings and the thoughts of the workers to carry out the tasks put before the entire Soviet people by the historic decisions of the 23rd Congress of our Party.

MYTHS, FANTASIES AND SHOW TRIALS:
ECHOES OF THE PAST

WILLIAM KOREY

E ARLY in the Twentieth Century there appeared a crude anti-Semitic work in Tsarist Russia which purported to be the *Protocols of the Elders of Zion*. It described the hidden and sinister plans of the all-powerful "Elders of Zion" to establish control over the world by fostering discontent within each state, then by discrediting governmental authorities and, finally, by exacerbating relations between states. A patent forgery composed of absurd allegations, the *Protocols*, nonetheless, took on a life of its own, was accepted in certain fashionable circles both in Russia and elsewhere, and eventually became what one scholar has called a "warrant for genocide."[1]

Exactly a half-century after the first edition of the *Protocols* was printed, a similar hoax was fabricated on the same soil but under a different regime. The "Doctors' Plot" of Joseph Stalin and Lavrenti Beria had conjured up an elaborate conspiracy of "Zionists" who planned the destruction of the Soviet state by the murder of its leaders. The principal mechanism of the Zionist plot was identified as the American Jewish Joint Distribution Committee — known generally as the "Joint" — a Jewish social relief and rehabilitation agency. Several months before the Doctors' Plot was unveiled to the Soviet public, a rehearsal of the conspiracy theme was held in Prague under instructions of the Soviet secret police. Rudolf Slansky, the Czech Party Secretary-General, and his associates were charged with being agents of the "Joint" and part of the world Zionist underground.

Later, after Stalin's death, the Doctors' Plot would be presented to the public as an aberration, a product of the dead dictator's paranoia. (His daughter, Svetlana Alliluyeva, many years later revealed that Stalin's hysterical suspicion about Zionism led him to warn her that her first husband, a Jew, had been insidiously "thrown your way by the Zionists.") But recent developments in the field of Soviet propaganda suggest that the fantasy conceptions concerning a Zionist conspiracy may be a reflection less of an individual's whim than of something endemic to reactionary Russian tradition. Fifteen years after the Doctors' Plot and 65 years after the *Protocols* appeared, the Soviet press and radio have shaped the contours of a newly-discovered Zionist plot that is disturbingly familiar.

A new dimension, however, has been added. If previous conceptions of the Zionist conspiracy were principally geared to domestic considerations, i.e., the need for a scapegoat upon which the ills of society can be heaped, the recent conception was linked to a foreign policy consideration: rationalization of the invasion of Czechoslovakia. Cloaking military intervention with some ideological justification is an inevitable function of the propaganda machinery of an aggressor state. What is extraordinary about the Soviet rationalization (as well as that of Poland and East Germany) is not so much the application of the concept of the "socialist commonwealth," the roots of which can be traced back to the early years of the Comintern, but rather the utilization of a myth that has a distinctively anti-Semitic character.

SOMETIME during late July 1967 a high-level decision was taken in Moscow to launch a massive internal and external propaganda campaign depicting Zionism as a major threat to the Communist world, the newly-independent states and the national-liberation movements. In the first week of August 1967 an article entitled "What is Zionism?" appeared simultaneously in the principal provincial organs of the USSR. Its opening paragraph struck the dominant note of the campaign: "A wide network of Zionist organizations with a common centre, a common program, and funds exceeding by far the funds of the Mafia 'Cosa Nostra' is active behind the scenes of the international theatre."

Stereotypic images of the Jew abound in the paranoid portrait sketched by the author. The global "Zionist Corporation" is composed of "smart dealers in politics and finance, religion and trade" whose "well-camouflaged aim" is the "enrichment by any means of the "international Zionist network." Exercising control over more than 1,000 newspapers and magazines in "very many countries of the world," with an "unlimited budget," the world Zionist "machine" services the vast monopolies of the West in their attempt "to establish control over the whole world."

If the campaign had its psychological roots in the dark phantasmagoric past, which had been nourished in the climate of Stalin's last years, it also served a pragmatic political purpose. With the Soviet Union's client Arab states suffering a major debacle in the Six-Day War and the Communist regime itself badly thwarted in its diplomatic endeavor at the United Nations to compel an Israeli withdrawal from occupied territory, a convenient scapegoat was needed to rationalize severe setbacks. Tiny Israel and public opinion were surely not the factors. The enemy must rather be presented as a hidden, all-powerful and perfidious international force, linked somehow with Israel. "World Zionism" was the ideological cloth that could be cut to fit the designated adversary. The citizenry of Communist states as well as those of the Arab and Afro-Asian world were literally saturated during the following months with this theme. Foreign radio broadcasts beamed from Moscow chattered away endlessly about Zionism as if this mysterious ghost would take on flesh by repeated incantation.

The flight from reality reached its nadir in the USSR in the fall and winter of 1967. In October, *Komsomolskaia pravda*, the mass circulation newspaper of the young Communist League, offered its readers a surrealistic description of the enemy: an "invisible but huge and mighty empire of financiers and industrialists," Zionism is the lackey "at the beck and call of the rich master whose nationality is exploitation and whose God is the dollar." With overwhelming economic and political power at its disposal, Zionism is able to exert "effective moral and psychological influence upon the sentiments and minds of people . . . in many countries." About a dozen countries are specifically mentioned but the author notes that the giant octopus commands "wide possibilities" in almost seventy countries of the globe.

Most notably subject to Zionist influence is the United States. To document his thesis, the author rattles off unusual data: the number of Zionists in America totals 20-25 million (there are but 6 million Jews in the U.S.); the percentage of Zionists among American lawyers is 70; the percentage of Zionists among physicists "including those engaged in secret work on the preparation of weapons for mass destruction" is 69; and the percentage of Zionists among industrialists is 43. Especially strong is Zionist influence in the mass media where its adherents own 80 per cent of the big publishing houses.

So extraordinarily precise was the Soviet published data that observers speculated about their source. Even a fantasy world draws upon elements of reality. Exhaustive research has finally unearthed the basis of the author's figures. It is an obscure pamphlet of 81 pages entitled *America — A Zionist Colony*, published in Cairo in 1957. The writer was a certain Saleh Dasuki who, besides specifying the percentages noted above, explained that "Jews, whether they have preserved their religion or whether they have adopted other religions, are known in the U.S.A. under the collective name of Zionists." Specialists in the field of hate propaganda recall that in 1957 Cairo had set up a veritable factory for the production of anti-Semitic literature. It operated under the direction of a former employee of Joseph Paul Goebbels' Nazi Propaganda Ministry, Johannes von Leers, who had adopted the Arabic name, Omar Amin.

Communist stalwarts were given further insights in December by a key Party organ, *Agitator*, which instructs activists on basic tactical guidelines. The author, Yurii Konstantinov, found the World Zionist Organization to be a "political, economic and military concern" with broad interests ranging from "religion to intelligence" and having at its disposal "extremely large funds" obtained from "Zionist multimillionaires." The influence of the Zionist operation is demonstrated by its alleged ownership or control of 1,036 newspapers and magazines published throughout the world. If this failed to stretch the credulity of the reader, the author retreated to the more conspiratorial warning: Zionists work hard to deliberately shield their influence from public view. *Agitator* advised Party activists that anti-Zionist propaganda would be accused of being anti-Semitic. But this, the journal emphasized, was a mere ploy, for the Zionist is the major purveyor of anti-Semitism.

A disturbing if not surprising feature of the propaganda campaign was the rehabilitation of the Soviet Union's leading purveyor of anti-Semitic bigotry, Trofim K. Kichko. His 1963 published book, *Judaism Without Embellishment*, was so vulgar and noxious in its language and illustrations that Communist parties everywhere joined a world-wide chorus of criticism demanding the withdrawal of the Soviet publication. In response, the Soviet Party's Ideological Commission condemned the book and it was removed from book-stalls while Kichko himself was ousted from the Party. But now he reappeared with an article in a Ukrainian Party youth organ which described a plot of "international Zionist bankers," including the Rockefellers, to transform the Middle East into "a strategic launching pad aimed against the socialist world, against the international workers' and liberation movements." Curiously, the Rockefellers appear in the writings of Kichko and his colleagues, just as they had in Nazi mythology, as the archetype of the Jewish banker. In January 1968 Kichko was awarded the highly-prized "certificate of honor" by the Supreme Soviet Praesidium of the Ukraine.

Having been duly honored, the Ukrainian "authority" on Judaism proceeded to write a new book, *Judaism and Zionism*, published in 1968 in Kiev. The edition was unusually large — 60,000 copies — and designed "for a wide circle of readers." Kichko's virulent bigotry is again made evident with his description of Judaism as a doctrine which teaches "thievery, betrayal and perfidy" as well as a "poisonous hatred for all other peoples." The ultimate objective of Judaism, it appears, is the fulfilment of God's promise that "the whole world belongs to the Jews." This doctrine, he argues, has been pressed into the service of Zionism in order to help it create a "World Jewish Power" in Palestine and to fulfil "the territorial-colonialist ambitions" of the "imperialist allies and admirers" of Zionism. Zionism, Kichko finds, is the reverse side of the coin of "cosmopolitanism," an ideology preaching that "the Fatherland of every person is not the country in which he is born, but the entire world." The author of the *Protocols* could not have found a more apt spiritual descendant than Kichko.

———

AT least in one area in the USSR the anti-Zionist propaganda had taken its toll. An unprecedented "appeal" to the Soviet Lithuanian Party, written in February 1968 by 26 Communist and non-Party representatives of the Jewish intelligentsia, declared that the newspaper campaign has "revived anti-Semitic passions in a certain part of the Lithuanian (and not only Lithuanian) people." It spelled out how "individual leading personalities, Communists," encouraged by the press, are "openly promoting" discrimination against Jews. The result, according to the 26 signers, is the virtual exclusion of Jews from political life and from the judicial and trade union apparatus. Jewish students are not given state scholarships to universities in Moscow and Leningrad, nor admitted to postgraduate institutes in those cities.[2] The authors concluded that the consequence of being "publicly insulted in the press," has been an increase in "emigrational tendencies" among Jews.

In the early summer of 1968 the theme of the world Zionist plot began to be employed in a new direction. The locus of Soviet concern was no longer only the Middle East where a scapegoat was needed to explain the failures of Soviet policy. The basic fear of the Communist leadership now centered on Czechoslovakia where the humanizing and democratic tendencies of the Alexander Dubcek leadership threatened to burst the integument of Soviet totalitarianism. World Zionism would now be depicted as the spearhead of international capitalism engaged in an effort to subvert Communist states and exacerbate relationships between them. (Similarity to the fundamental elements of the old *Protocols* is here expecially marked.)

An article in the authoritative foreign policy journal *Mezhdunarod-naia zhizn'*, published in June 1968, signalled the change in emphasis of the Zionist theme. Entitled "Israel, Zionism and International Imperialism," the article was written by a leading Soviet "expert" on the subject of Zionism, K. Ivanov. He recapitulated the international conspiracy thesis, linking world Zionism, Jewish capitalism, Israel, American imperialism and West German revanchism in a gigantic plot to overthrow Communist rule. Since Western imperialism is unable to destroy by military means the Communist states of Eastern Europe, he argued, it has been forced to rely upon ideological subversion. The key role is played by world Zionists who "are trying to instill into the minds of Jews in various countries, including the socialist countries, that they have a 'dual citizenship' — one, a secondary one, in the country of actual domicile, and the other, the basic, spiritual and religious one, in Israel."

The potential enemy was clear: a "fifth column" of Jews who have fallen prey to the "dual citizenship" concept. Ivanov charged that the imperialist intelligence services and psychological warfare agencies were spending hundreds of millions of dollars, utilizing the dual citizenship concept, to "subvert and corrupt" the "fraternal militant community of the socialist countries." The target of the subverters and corrupters, it was apparent, was Czechoslovakia.

In August, just a few days before the Soviet invasion of Czechoslovakia, leading Soviet organs, including the important Defense Ministry newspaper *Krasnaia zvezda* as well as *Komsomolskaia pravda* dealt at length with mysterious "saboteurs" who threaten to undermine the socialist commonwealth. Judaism was singled out for condemnation as prescribing "racial exclusivism" and as justifying "crimes against 'Gentiles.'" Woven into this warped fabric of thought were such characteristic threads as the sinister role of "Joint," the danger of the dual citizenship concept, the challenge of the international Zionist conspiracy.

Specific public identification of the names of the "saboteurs" might have proved unseemly at the time. But Moscow, already during July, had set Czechoslovakia and the world on notice as to whom it regarded as the culprits desecrating the Communist image: Eduard Goldstuecker, chairman of the Union of Writers and vice-rector of Charles University; Frantisek Kriegel, Politburo member and chairman of the National Front; Ota Sik, Deputy Premier and the leading economic reformer; and Bohumil Lomsky, Minister of Defense. All were considered to be Jews (although Sik has emphasized that he is not).

Kriegel was to receive personal Soviet attention. He was included in the top leadership group that met in Moscow with the Soviet authorities. Soviet Premier Alexei Kosygin is reported to have refused point-blank to negotiate with Kriegel, snarling, "What is the Jew doing here?" Bertrand Russell in a letter to *The Times* of London on September 16 revealed that Kriegel had been subjected to "vicious treatment" in Moscow. It is believed that the Russians wanted to prevent his return to Prague but President Ludwik Svoboda refused to budge unless Kriegel was allowed to come back with his colleagues. Unlike the other top Czech officials, Kriegel's signature is absent from the Moscow agreement.

NO sooner had the Soviet troops crossed the Czech frontier than official Soviet organs were set to work to portray Czechoslovakia as the embodiment of a "counter-revolution" in which secret Zionists played a decisive role. On August 23, the Government newspaper *Izvestiia* described an omnipresent "counter-revolutionary underground" that included at its core the Club of Non-Party Activists (KAN). The Soviet newspaper charged that three of its leaders — Rybacek, Musil and Klementjev — were "agents of the international Zionist organization, 'Joint.'" Aside from the fact that the "Joint" has not functioned in Czechoslovakia for twenty years, none of the three "agents" was Jewish.

The next day, a Moscow English-language broadcast to Africa contended that "Zionist elements" had taken control of the Czech information organs and were demanding the establishment of friendly relations with Israel. Listeners were also told that these "'elements' refuse to support the struggle of the Africans against racism and colonialism in Africa."

The official *White Book* on the invasion, a documentary volume published on September 10 by Moscow and distributed widely in several languages (the authors were identified as the "Press Group of Soviet Journalists"), reiterated the theme that KAN was led by agents of international Zionism. It went on to add that an important reason for the intervention of the Warsaw Pact powers was the effort by certain forces "to bring about a change in Czechoslovakia's position with regard to the unanimous condemnation by the Socialist countries of Israel's aggression, and, in particular, to restore diplomatic relations with that country."

The theme of a conspiracy threatening Czechoslovakia was carried into 1969. In March, Tass reproduced in detail a lengthy story which had appeared in a Lebanese Communist newspaper, *Al Dunia*. The story disclosed the decision of a "secret meeting" that had somehow escaped the attention of the world press:

> A secret meeting has recently been held in London. Taking part in it were representatives of the biggest Zionist organizations and supporters of the so-called "United Organiza-

tion of Czech and Slovak Politicians Inside and Outside Czechoslovakia.

The plot involved Jews within Czechoslovakia who held "responsible posts" in political, economic and cultural spheres, and who maintained "strong contacts with Zionism." The purpose was nothing less than the overthrow of the socialist system in that country and the restoration of capitalism. The Tass dispatch was carried in all the leading Soviet organs and on Moscow Radio.

If the campaign against Zionism served the opportunistic function of justifying the application of brute force, it also reflected a deep-seated anti-Semitism in some sectors of the Soviet leadership. Especially revealing of this bigotry was a major *Izvestiia* story of September 4, 1968. It purported to be an expose of the Czech Foreign Minister Jiri Hajek, who had courageously flown to the United Nations on the occasion of the invasion to present his country's desperate situation before the Security Council. To the *Izvestiia* editors and their masters, seeking a Zionist label to pin upon the unreconstructed Hajek, it must have seemed natural that he was of Jewish origin. The article, besides describing a lurid past of Hajek—the details of which were pure concoction—emphasized that he had "changed his name some time ago from Karpeles to Hajek." Karpeles is a characteristic Jewish name among East Central Europeans.

The deliberate malice turned out to be an indelicate journalistic boner for, as *Volksstimme*, organ of the Austrian Communist Party, revealed shortly afterwards, *Izvestiia* had confused Jiri Hajek with another Hajek whose first name was Bedrich and who had previously been "Karpeles." The Czech Foreign Minister had not changed his name and he was not Jewish. Hajek was later to comment to the liberal Czech journal *Reporter*: "I should like to emphasize that I would not be ashamed to be a Jew because I think that in this country we discarded racism some time ago." But the boner offers a telling insight into what "research" information the Soviets relied upon for its campaign against Zionism.

MOSCOW'S charges about a world Zionist conspiracy were echoed by the other major Warsaw Pact powers, Poland and East Germany (although not by Hungary and Bulgaria). Official Polish propaganda took as its point of departure the student uprisings in various Polish cities during March 1968, and went on to relate these developments, ascribed to Zionist forces, to events in Czechoslovakia. The principal spokesman of Poland on the subject was General Jan Czapla, deputy head of the Political Administration in the Polish Ministry of Defense. In an article in *Trybuna Ludu* on August 25 (and later carried on Warsaw Radio as well as in the Polish

Army journal), General Czapla stated that "revisionist and Zionist forces" — the "international bridgehead of imperialism" — had developed to such a point in Czechoslovakia as "to menace directly and effectively the foundations of socialism and strike directly at Communists." In Poland, on the other hand, he declared, these forces had been crushed. And, of course, it was necessary to do the same in Czechoslovakia.

The Soviet analyst, K. Ivanov, supported the Czapla juxtaposition of the Polish events and developments in Czechoslovakia. In a comprehensive discussion of the steps leading up to and justifying the military intervention, published in *Mezhdunarodnaia zhizn'* in October, Ivanov noted that among the "necessary lessons to be drawn" was that counterrevolution has an attraction for "definite strata of the population." Just as in Poland in the spring of 1968, "Right-wing bourgeois, Zionist trends" came to the surface, so too in Czechoslovakia, Zionists, along with Trotskyites(!), anarcho-syndicalists, and Rightists made themselves manifest.

Walter Ulbricht's propaganda machine in East Germany went even further than either the Soviet or Polish press. If the latter two found that the Zionists were but threatening the foundations of Czech Communism, *Neues Deutschland* argued that "the workers have lost control over the Communist Party of Czechoslovakia, and Zionist forces have taken over the leadership of the Party." The statement appeared on August 25, precisely the same day that General Czapla's article was published in *Trybuna Ludu*. The orchestration of the propaganda effort couldn't have been clearer. Two days earlier *Izvestiia* had launched the official justification for the Warsaw Pact powers.

The more virulent character of the campaign against Zionism in the East German mass media, both during the Czech crisis and going back to the post-Six Day War period, raised an intriguing question which has been closely studied by Simon Wiesenthal, the celebrated hunter of former Nazis. In a press conference on September 6, he told correspondents in Vienna that there was a "great difference in tone between East Germany and the other East bloc states" in the public treatment of the supposed threat of Zionism. He discovered that "the expressions, terms and ideological categories of thought" employed in the East German press and radio were "much more strongly reminiscent" of the *Voelkischer Beobachter, Stuermer* and *Schwarze Korps* than of Communist organs. Wiensenthal did not find this accidental: 39 persons who had occupied influential posts during the Nazi era, today have "at least the same influence in the press, radio, and the propaganda organs of East Germany." [3]

THERE can be little doubt now but that the campaign against world Zionism was to have been climaxed with a staged show trial, reminiscent of those of the early '50s. Both *Le Monde* on September 12 and *The Times* of London on September 13 carried an article written by a prominent Czech Communist which disclosed that the Soviets were insisting than an "anti-Zionist trial must be staged, starring Mr. Kriegel and Professor Eduard Goldstuecker." The author further stated that Moscow was prepared to "produce evidence" for such a trial within three months. Additional confirmation came from Bertrand Russell in his letter to *The Times* on September 16. On the basis of "excellent authority," he was convinced that the Soviets were "pressing for a trial in the classic Stalinist tradition of the 'Doctors' Plot' " in order to divert attention from the aggression in Czechoslovakia.

A speech delivered by Dubcek on October 11, carried in both press and on radio but scarcely noted in the West, strongly suggested that he was vigorously resisting pressure for a staged show trial. The address was devoted to a report on his negotiations with the Soviet Union, held the previous week in Moscow, during which he was compelled to accede to wide-ranging demands upon Czech freedom. While cataloguing the humiliating concessions, Dubcek digressed to observe that there are "those who believe the moment is propitious for a return to the practises of the 1950s." The allusion to the notorious Slansky trial was all too clear.

Had the show trial been held, the central figure of the proceedings *in absentia* would no doubt have been Professor Goldstuecker, currently teaching at the University of Sussex in England. The Soviet press has been replete with more abuse hurled upon him than any other Czech reformer. *Literaturnaia gazeta* on October 2 devoted special attention to him, giving emphasis to his Jewish origin. After noting that Goldstuecker had been an "active member" of a Zionist youth organization when he was a teenager, the periodical recalled that he had been appointed by Czechoslovakia as its ambassador to Israel. The article then curiously reminded its readers of an earlier show trial: "But after one year he was recalled; trials in Czechoslovakia had already begun of a number of public figures accused of criminal contacts with world Zionism."

As late as December 1968 the theme of anti-Semitism continued. *Zpravy,* the Russian occupation newspaper published in the Czech language, carried stories having a "marked anti-Semitic flavour." [4] Yet, the Soviet propaganda effort was having little, if any, effect within Czechoslovakia. On the contrary, it evoked the sharpest condemnation from workers and intellectuals, expressed in various forums and in the news media. A comment on "racial prejudice" in the journal *Politika* (October 24) summed up Czech reaction:

> We have had tragic experiences with all sorts of pogroms, whether organized by Hitler or initiated by people who 17 years ago prepared the political trials. That is why we are so sensitive about any anti-Semitic attack.

No doubt, sophisticated Russians would react in the same way to ancient myths, were they free to express themselves. But the current crop of Soviet leaders still draw sustenance from out-dated fantasies that are consonant with historic prejudices.

During 1969, the official Soviet mass media continued and intensified its drumbeat about omnipotent Zionist power. The trade union journal *Sovietskiie profsoiuzy*, in its January issue, accused Zionism of inciting the Polish youth uprisings of the previous year and of exerting a "disintegrating influence" upon Czechoslovak youth. The entire thrust of Zionism, the author argued, was the use of Jewish citizens in all capitalist countries to conduct "subversive work" against the USSR and to "undermine from within" the friendship of the various Soviet peoples. A Soviet newspaper that specializes in anti-Zionist diatribes, *Sovietskaia Rossiia*, carried on January 24 a long expose which focused upon Zionism's "provocative and treacherous" propaganda campaign to convince Jews that they have a "dual loyalty."

In February, the mass circulation weekly *Ogonek* underscored the massive threat of the Zionists. Having at their disposal vast resources, the Zionists "infiltrated their agents into the press, the radio, the television and the cinema of all States." The impact of that "infiltration" was spelled out in various foreign broadcasts by Moscow Radio during March: encouragement of counter-revolution during "the last ten years" in Hungary, Poland and Czechoslovakia; support of "subversive activities in African countries"; the propagation of militant anti-communist and chauvinist propaganda.

THE climax of the campaign was the publication of an extraordinary book (75,000 copies) titled *Beware: Zionism!* Written by Yuri Ivanov, it weaves together into 173 pages the various strands of the anti-Zionist theme spun over the course of the past three years. Zionism is presented as a giant international "Concern" which might appropriately be titled "world 'Ministry' on the affairs of 'World Jewry.' " With "one of the largest amalgamations of capital" available to it, the "Ministry" maintains an extensive "international intelligence centre" and a "well-organized service for misinformation and propaganda." The objective of the "Concern's" various "departments" which operate under a "single management" is "profit and enrichment" aimed at safeguarding "its power." Details of international Zionism's influence on the policy of Israel, which it considers as its own "property," as well as its cunning efforts aimed at subverting both the socialist and new national states are spelled out. Elaborated, too, is the ramified network of Zionist propaganda organs buttressed by the major mass media which have been "penetrated" by "sympathizing elements."

The significance of this obsessive and irrational work might ordinarily be minimized as an isolated literary phenomenon were it not for the fact that its publication was accompanied by a synchronized campaign of laudatory reviews in almost all the major Soviet newspapers and magazines, and in broadcasts by *Tass* in numerous foreign languages. The voice of the official Soviet authority was not disguised. It spoke clearly through *Pravda* (March 9):

> From the pages of Yu. Ivanov's book emerges the true and evil image of Zionism and this constitutes the undoubted importance of the book.

With the ideology of the Ivanov book so strongly endorsed, Soviet journalists could feel free to give vent to the wildest concoctions. Thus. V. Vysotsky, writing on May 31, 1969, in Byelorussia's leading newspaper, *Sovetskaia Byelorossia*, "discovered" that a secret meeting of Zionists had taken place in London in 1968 at which it was decided to take over the entire Arab world—Lebanon, Syria, Jordan, Iraq, Yemen, Saudi Arabia and the Arab peninsula. From this base, Vysotsky went on, the Zionists planned to attain "mastery over mankind" using all possible devices—"force, bribery, slyness, perfidy, subversion and espionage."

The themes of the "Protocols" continued into 1970. The newspaper of the Ministry of Defense, *Krasnaia Zvezda*, on March 13, observed that the Zionists "are making wide use out of their agents in dozens of countries throughout the world . . . to mobilize the Jews of all countries" in order to serve Israel. The same Ministry, ten days later, published in an extraordinary edition of 200,000 copies a novel by Ivan Shevtsov called *Love and Hate*. The central character in this second novel by Shevtsov is a Jew presented as a pervert, sadist, dope peddler and killer. Not to be outdone, the Party's principal organ for propagandists, *Agitator*, warned in March that the Zionists are attempting, through radio and "other means of communication," to "brainwash Soviet citizens of Jewish origin." The warning to Soviet Jews couldn't have been more explicit.

1970 was also marked by the publication of a revised edition of Ivanov's *Beware: Zionism!*, lengthy passages of which especially concerning the House of Rothschild, were widely reprinted in the Soviet press. The Rothschilds, as in Nazi propaganda, were portrayed as the centerpiece of the world Zionist conspiracy. The family became symbolic of a "Jewish world government," with its funds transferred secretly out of France to a Tel Aviv bank. The new edition was especially noteworthy for presenting the Vatican and the Ecumenical Council as instruments of the "Jewish Millionaires' Conspiracy."

It was in the context of this massive propaganda campaign against Zionism that the Soviet authorities arrested 34 Jews in various parts of the country beginning on June 15, 1970. The pretext was an alleged hijacking plot by a number of Jews from Riga, but the transparent objective was to intimidate the Jewish community and bring a halt to the applications and petitions of the growing number of Jews desirous of emigrating to Israel. As one young Leningrad Jew, Viktor Boguslavsky, wrote: "Their only crime was that they were born Jews and they sought to remain Jews." He too was arrested. Twelve, including two non-Jews, who were brought to trial in December 1970 and January 1971, received long prison terms. Two condemned to death had their sentences commuted to 15 years after a world-wide outcry protesting the severity of the penalties.

The fantasy world of the ancient *Protocols of the Elders of Zion,* clearly, continues to display a remarkable vitality in present day Soviet Russia. The prominent German Marxist, August Bebel, once commented that anti-Semitism is the "socialism of fools." The later Stalinist period and more recent Soviet activities indicate that this form of socialism is not alien to Russian tradition.

---

[1] Norman Cohn, *Warrant for Genocide* (New York: Harper & Row, 1966).

[2] It was in neighboring Poland that the impact of the anti-Zionist campaign was massively felt. Here the political objective was less the rationalization of the Communist role in the Middle East conflict as it was the determination to crush the rising revolt of Polish students and intellectuals. Jews (or Zionists) could be offered as scapegoats for the accumulating discontent and growing alienation. Professor Adam Schaff, Poland's great Marxist philosopher, in an important work published in 1965, had warned that "the chief racist danger in our society . . . is represented by anti-Semitism. . . ." Now he and his associates would feel its full force as scapegoating became a major factor in an intense factional struggle for power.

[3] One curious and, as yet unexplained, feature of the Zionist propaganda campaign against Czechoslovakia was a crude forgery of a letter attributed to Wiesenthal which was circulated in Prague in May 1968. It called upon "friends in Czechoslovakia" to fight for "progressive processes" and thereby bring about conditions that will result in "restoring friendly relations between Israel and Czechoslovakia." The object of the forgery was provocatory.

[4] *The Times* (London), December 2, 1968

SELECTIONS FROM SOVIET PUBLICATIONS AND MASS MEDIA

FROM *Sovietskiye Profsoyuzy*, No. 2, January 1969:

Today [the Zionists] undertake measures to exert an ideologically harmful influence on the politically immature part of the youth—as, for instance, in the period of the Poznan incidents in Poland in 1956. Zionist groups that existed in the University of Warsaw, in the Polytechnic Institute and in other institutes of learning, were engaged in constant incitement of the students. It was also not without the participation of the Zionist centres that the incidents of March 1968 took place in the Polish People's Republic. The Zionists had exerted their disintegrating influence on the youth of the Czechoslovak Socialist Republic as well. In the period of the existence in Moscow of the Israeli diplomatic representation, the Zionist organizations and Israeli intelligence mainly relied on the official workers of the Embassy and on tourists from Israel for the conduct of subversive work against our country. After the breaking off of the diplomatic relations between the Soviet Union and Israel, the Israeli intelligence and Zionist organizations are using Jews—citizens of other capitalist countries—for the conduct of subversive work against the U.S.S.R. . . . to undermine from within the fraternal friendship of the peoples of the U.S.S.R.—one of the foundations of the might of our Socialist State. Communism, socialism, friendship of peoples and their unity with the Communist Party of the Soviet Union and the Soviet Government—all this sticks in the throats of the Zionists.

FROM *Tass*, Moscow Radio, March 6, 1969:

A secret meeting has recently been held in London. Taking part in it were representatives of the biggest Zionist organizations and supporters of the so-called United International Organization of Czech and Slovak Politicians Inside and Outside Czechoslovakia, the Lebanese newspaper *Al Dunia* reports, in a dispatch from London. The newspaper points out that Israel and international Zionism were always closely watching the development in Czechoslovakia since January 1968. They tried not only to get exact data about everything going on in that country, but to exert active influence on the development of events in Czechoslovakia. Tel Aviv attained a certain success in this. Tel Aviv knew about the subjects of discussion in the Czechoslovak leadership and about the talks with foreign representatives, including those between Soviet and Czechoslovak leaders in Cierna-on-Tisa. It turned out to be possible because many Jews residing in Czechoslovakia maintain strong contacts with Zionism and with the "great Israel movement," the dispatch says. Many of them hold responsible posts in the political, scientific and cultural spheres and are in favour of toppling the socialist system in Czechoslovakia, and the restoration there of a capitalist system that would be in keeping with Israel's interests. The article quotes passages from the European Zionist magazine *Jewish Observer and Middle East Review* . . . Israel, as well as Zionist organizations in the United States and the West European countries, have allocated huge sums to finance internal opposition in Czechoslovakia. It is not surprising, therefore, the newspaper continues, that Zionism supports the actions of Czechoslovak anti-communist groupings outside the country and strives to create, with the active participation of Zionists, a united organization called People's Assembly. *Al Dunia* says that, according to information received from Czechoslovak refugees, the London meeting was attended by new emigres, including Brodsky, former president of the 231 Club which has been outlawed in Czechoslovakia. It is also known that the meeting was attended by representatives of Czechoslovakia's political opposition such as O. Sik and E. Goldstuecker who have broad international contacts with, among others, Zionist organizations all over the world. The meeting's participants reached agreement to establish contacts with groups and individuals both inside Czechoslovakia and outside the country.

FROM *Moscow Radio*, October 15, 1969:

It appears from Golda Meir's biography that as far back as 1948 she went overseas to establish contact with all American Zionists, and primarily with the financial wizards whose contributions to the United Jewish Appeal, the Zionist organization whose task is to collect funds for Israel, were the most generous. In June 1967, immediately after Israel's aggression against Arab countries began, the United Jewish Appeal called for donations: by 14 August 1967 it had collected 500 million dollars. Now this organization is selling 1,000 million dollars' worth of Israeli State bonds in the USA. The US Government, openly encouraging this campaign, has passed the unprecedented decision to exempt this sum from taxation. The colossal sums amassed by the Zionists with the aid of the biggest American bankers and monopolists of Jewish origin, Rothschild, Rockefeller and others, enable them to exert great influence among the people of the USA. The combined circulation of the Zionist magazines published in English is several tens of millions of copies. The extent to which these brainwashing efforts are successful is shown by the following fact: the *Washington Post* has admitted that only one American in 12 believes that the Israelis were the first to attack the Arabs in June 1967. The opinion of Zionist organizations and the bankers and monopolists who support them is never disregarded by Washington's most influential circles.

FROM *Radianska Ukraina* [Kiev daily], July 30, 1969:

CRIME AS INSTRUMENT OF POLICY
(THE SECRET BECOMES KNOWN)

By V. Savtsov

History repeats itself. The Zionist leaders in Russia, as early as the next day after the Great October Socialist Revolution, had called upon their organizations to fight against the Soviet rule. Since then, the main objects of the insinuations and of the subversive activities of international Zionism (in the strategic sense) have been and remain the following: the Soviet Union, the other states of the Socialist Concord, the international communist and workers' movement and the national-liberation struggle of the peoples. This thesis has been stressed, with great forwardness and conviction, by the Moscow International Conference of Communist and Workers' Parties.

The Zionists from the Israeli Intelligence Service disdain nothing. Their arsenal contains: direct recruiting of Soviet citizens (only recently several diplomats and "tourists" have been expelled for such activities from the Soviet Union, and from our Republic in particular), the criminal, full of hostile insinuations propaganda of the "Voice of Israel," the thrusting on of a correspondence from outside of a non-innocent and later frequently of an espionage character, the sending of mail packages with anti-Soviet literature and, here and there, direct provocations as well. In particular, in the years 1966-1968, International Zionism became one of the moving forces behind the anti-socialist manifestations in Poland and in Czechoslovakia.

FROM *Kommunist Moldavii* [Kishinev monthly], June 1969:

THE INTRIGUES OF INTERNATIONAL
ZIONISM IN THE NEAR EAST

By I. Feldman

The main organizer and the idological center of Zionism is the World Zionist Organization, established in 1897. It is constructed on racial principles and is based in the USA. Possessing financial funds equal to the funds of the largest monopolistic amalgamations in the world, the Zionist organization controls and directs the activities of Zionist amalgamations in over 60 countries. The World Jewish Congress, which has its bases in 67 countries throughout the world, is in effect a branch of the World Zionist Organization. Besides these two largest Zionist organizations, there operate numerous societies, clubs, committees, unions and amalgamations.

At the head of the executive committee of the World Zionist Organization are the henchmen of the largest American monopolists of Jewish origin. Being one of the greatest owners in the modern capitalist world, the international Zionist corporation in effect controls the entire economy of Israel and regards Israel not only as its creation, but also as its property. This is why it strives to turn Israel into a militant beast of prey, to consolidate it as the ideological and political center controlling millions of Jews—citizens of the most varied countries of the world—and to strengthen its positions as a mediator in the cause of the economic and political penetration of imperialism into the developing countries of Africa and Asia.

The struggle against internationalism, the desire to raise an impenetrable wall between Jews and non-Jews and to impede the fraternal union of the workers of the entire world in their struggle against imperialism—these are the most important ideological foundations of Zionism.

The "orthodox" Zionist leaders of Israel remain deaf to the most acute problems of our times; they come out against the concord of the socialist states, against the international communist and workers' movement, and wage a struggle against the national-liberation movement of the peoples. They are ready to risk the fate of the peoples of the entire world, just to attain their narrowly mercenary aims—the isolation of Jewry and establishment of control over it.

FROM *Beward Zionism!* by Yuri Ivanov. Moscow: Political
Literature Publishing House, 1969:

Appearing against the socialist camp, international communism and the workers' movement, Zionism also fights against the national-liberation movement of peoples. One of the recent concrete actions in this direction was the aggression of the Israeli militarists against the Arab countries in June 1967.

By its military result this aggression has basically made an impression on two categories of persons: on citizens of a number of countries, traditionally limited and not very bright and on the revengists of Bonn whose unfulfilled dream had been and has remained a blitzkrieg.

But the absolute majority of people who refused to slide over the surface of events, was confronted—in view of the tragedy unfolded in the Near East—by the necessity to find an answer to a number of vital questions. Who were the forces that could have ensured at first the semblance of an Israel fighting single-handed against a whole group of Arab countries? Who managed, in good time, to work on a certain part of public opinion in a number of western countries and the USA in favor of the Israeli militarists? Who did the intelligence work and disclosed a number of military and political secrets of the Arabs? Who kept top secret the numerous financial and military deals of Israel? Etc.

Understandably, these comprehensive and manifold activities greatly exceed the possibilities of the Israeli secret service and of its propaganda apparatus. It is evident that there must have been a cooperation between the Israeli militarists and the ruling circles of the imperalist powers. But this answer however correct in principle, is not sufficient. (Official French propaganda for instance, did not have the possibility, during the aggression, of influencing public opinion in the country in a pro-Israeli spirit, on account of De Gaulle's foreign policy. This was done by the branches of the World Zionist Organization in France.) It is necessary to complement it by a conclusion about the existence of a connecting link which has practically and secretly ensured the manifold preparations of the latest Israeli expansion—the attempts to overthrow the progressive regimes in the UAR and Syria. The international Zionist alliance served as this connecting link, playing the role of a secret channel between the most reactionary forces in the imperialist states, first of all the USA, then the FRG and England and the Israeli militarists.

However, to reduce the significance of international Zionism in the Near East conflict to the role of a connecting link alone would be inaccurate. If one wants to visualize, in a most general way, the scheme of dependence of the main participants in the aggression, it would look approximately like this: Israeli militarists—international Zionism—the imperialist circles of the West headed by the USA.

The International Zionist Organization is economically connected by the closest of ties to the monopolies of the biggest imperialist powers, the USA first and foremost. Like the USA monopolies, the Zionist concern has long had a wide circle of "business interests" in the Near East. This is why its role in the Near East is not at all limited to that of a messenger boy. The Zionist concern appeared as an "employer" in relation to Israel's ruling circles, but in relation to the American monopolies it played the role of not the smallest partner by far in the sharing of the gangster loot.

The "six-day war" was not the first and is probably not the last adventure of international Zionism (the range of its interests is not limited to the region of the Suez Canal). However, the June 1967 aggression constituted this really rare occurrence when international Zionism, breaking its own firmly and long established rule, raised itself a little from behind the ramparts: Premier Levi Eshkol babbled out the amount put freely at the disposal of the Israeli ruling circles in the very first days of the war, by the Zionist organizations;. in Israel, an international consultation of millionaires of Jewish origin was openly convened; to the surprise of their fellow citizens, Zionists in a number of countries widely celebrated the victory of the Israeli armed forces. But this is only a rare episode in the history of the activities of the international Zionist concern. As a rule, it acts in an entirely different manner.

Here it is necessary to digress. According to our conviction, the assertion that any nation, nationality or national group "had suffered more than anyone in the world during the entire history of mankind," means not only a deliberate distortion of the facts of the past for the sake of base, nationalist aspiration, but also a deliberate undertaking of the positions of a racism that is merely turned inside out, and the instilling of open or hidden hostility toward all and the sowing of disunity.

It is precisely this path that has been purposefully chosen by the Zionist leaders in striving, in the interest of the exploiters, to gather under the Biblical banner of the "God-punished but also God-chosen nation" the multi-millionaires, the Poliakovs, the Oppenheimers and the Rothschilds, together with the Jewish workers and artisans, and so to place the Jewish workers in opposition to the non-Jewish workers.

The formation of the "Jewish State" has always been considered by the Zionist leaders not as their aim, but as an instrument for attaining different, much wider aims: the establishment of control over the Jewish masses, general enrichment for the sake of power, and the parasitical prosperity and the defence and consolidation of imperialism.

[59]

From *Judaism and Zionism* by T. K. Kichko. Kiev: Society
Znannia of the Ukrainian SSR, 1969:

Covering themselves by the teachings of Judaism, propagating the creation of one above-class Jewish State, the leaders of Zionism are trying to
prove that the Jews of all countries are allegedly "one Jewish nation," are
propagating class cooperation and are distracting the attention of working
Jews from a joint class struggle with the peoples of the countries in which
they live against their own and foreign oppressors, and from the struggle
for democratic freedom and peace.

By slanderous fabrications about the persecution of the Jews and of the
Jewish religion in the Soviet Union and in other socialist countries, the Zionists, together with the ideologists of imperialism, are trying to becloud the
consciousness of the working Jews and to paralyze their will for fighting for
socialism and communism, and are conducting propaganda directed at un-
dermining the unity of the peoples of socialist countries.

In their struggle against the ideas of communism, the Zionists have taken
up as their arms not only the ideology of the Jewish bourgeois nationalism,
but also cosmopolitanism and even antisemitism — masking all this by the
teachings of Judaism.

Not the least role in the imperialist and racist plans of the Zionists is
played by the reactionary dogmas of the Judaist teaching about the "God-
chosenness" of the Jewish people, its superiority over other peoples of the
world, about the "promised land," the future coming of the mythical Mes-
siah and others.

The morality of Judaism is not connected with the real needs and interests of the people. Moreover, it is contrary to their interests, is a certain man-
ifestation of individualism and of egoism which are characteristic of antago-
nistic society. Judaism cannot be a model of morality because on one side it
threatens people with "divine punishment" for sins and, on the other hand,
it itself sanctifies sins if they are in the interests of religion and of the exploiting classes.

Isn't the anti-humanism of Judaism best illustrated by the morality of
the prophet Moses himself? About this "most meek and holy Man" it is said
in the Torah that by his deeds he had brought about the loss of thousands of
Egyptians, while the Jews had been brought by him into the desert where
they were on the edge of death: "As soon as they begin rebelling against his
instructions, he commits the most cruel deeds against them in the name of
God. He kills them by thousands: by mass killings he brings them to sub-
jugation; he binds them hand and foot and gives them to be preys to
tyranny and victims of the extortion of the priests; that is, of his own family
and tribe. Under the banner of religion he inculcates the Israelites with
poisonous hatred for all other peoples; he obliges them to be inhuman,
haters of man and blood-thirsty; he teaches them thievery, betrayal and
perfidy; he orders them to usurp the lands of the Canaanites, persuading
them that God had promised these lands to their forefathers."

In the Torah it is also told that while Moses was talking with God on the
Mount of Sinai, his brother, the Levite Aaron, submitted to the demands of
the Israelites and made them an idol, which the Jews began to adore. When
he descended from the Mountain, Moses became angry. He rebuked his
brother for the "sin" committed, while, as concerns the people, this prophet

ordered the Levites to annihilate a thousand Israelites in order to atone by their blood for the evil.

Judaism calls on man to reconcile himself with difficult conditions of life, because "God's ways are inscrutable." It accustoms man to the idea that on earth there is not and there cannot be justice, that misfortunes, evil, wars and the killing of millions of people occur at the will of Yahve himself. There is a direct connection between this morality of Judaism and what the Israeli Zionists are doing in practice. Wasn't it according to the Torah that the Israeli extremists acted during the latest aggression against the Arab countries? Aren't they directed by religious teachings when they commit new provocations in the Near East?

SOVIET FOREIGN POLICY AND ANTI-SEMITISM

JOHN A. ARMSTRONG

THERE are few, if any, aspects of Soviet foreign policy which are more closely linked to Soviet internal affairs than is anti-Semitism. Before proceeding to an analysis of the motivation for anti-Semitism in Soviet foreign policy, however, we might consider certain additional evidence on the *group solidarity* of Jews in the USSR, a factor which is both interesting in itself and significant as a background element in Soviet policy.

By fortunate coincidence, very recently highly important statistical data indirectly related to the same point have been published in the USSR. Let us hope that this is just the beginning of a more abundant flow of quantitative evidence on the situation of Soviet Jewry. It is rather surprising, however, that even the available quantitative data and other sociological evidence on Jews in Russia have been little analyzed by Western social scientists, even in comparison with other aspects of Tsarist and Soviet society. Perhaps one of the most useful projects toward understanding the present plight of Soviet Jewry would be a thorough sociological analysis of the Jewish communities under the Tsars—a difficult but by no means impossible task.

The new statistics on Soviet Jews constitute a small section of M. V. Kurman and I. V. Lebedinskii, *Naselenie Bol'shogo Sotsialisticheskogo Goroda (The Population of a Large Soviet City)*, published last year in Moscow by the specialized publishing house Statistika. The data relate only to Kharkov, but would seem to be fairly representative for Jews in the USSR as a whole. Kharkov lies outside the old Pale region which was the center of traditional Jewish culture; thus its Jewish community bears certain resemblance to the newer, large communities in Moscow and Leningrad. On the other hand, Kharkov has very probably had a large influx from the dispersed Pale communities since Civil War terrorism and especially since World War II. The data is restricted to 1960. Assuming, however, that this year was not deliberately selected by the Soviet authors as unrepresentative (and the context of the work makes this seem unlikely), the data may be regarded as a "sample" sufficiently large to permit significant inferences.

At first glance, the figures in Table I might suggest that, since the proportion of Jews marrying outside their own ethnic group is only a little smaller than that of Russians and Ukrainians; *i.e.*, that ethnic solidarity among the three groups is similar in intensity. Since, however, the Jews (in contrast to the two dominant ethnic groups) are a tiny minority in Kharkov's population, a more significant calculation is the ratio of actual Jewish endogamous (intra-group) marriages to the number of exogamous (mixed) marriages which could be statistically expected if Jews chose their marriage partners in the city on a purely random basis. (The calculation is slightly imprecise because it must be based on total ethnic populations rather than on prime marriageable age-groups, for which Soviet data is not available.)

There are, of course, two ways in which the greatly superior degree of endogamy among Jews (as compared to major Kharkov ethnic groups) can be accounted for. Conceivably Jews may *have* to marry within their own group because others (mainly in the dominant groups) refuse to enter into marriage with them. In fact, however, what evidence there is points the opposite way. In Leningrad, Jews who choose the highly atypical "Soviet style" wedding at the "Palace of Marriages" have overwhelmingly non-Jewish spouses (even there, though, the endogamy ratio is higher than would be produced by purely random choice). Furthermore, the official Soviet position is in favor of exogamous marriage: as Kurman and Lebidinskii put it, "the process of drawing together of nations in the USSR is especially demonstrated by observing the question of men and women of different nationalities entering into marriage." Hearsay evidence concerning the views of at least better-educated Soviet city-dwellers also suggests that there is no widespread antipathy to marrying Jews. One is led, therefore, to reject the possibility that Jewish endogamy is involuntary; the remaining explanation—strongly in accord with Mr. Decter's evidence—is that Jews marry

[63]

Table I. MARRIAGES IN KHARKOV—1960

Nationality of Bride	Nationality of Bridegroom			Ethnically Exogamous Bridegrooms		
	Russian	*Ukrainian*	*Jewish*	*TOTAL BRIDEGROOMS* *[incl. misc.]*	*[No.]*	*[%]*
Russian	2,188	2,423	86	4,777	2,589	54.2
Ukrainian	2,241	3,643	72	6,016	2,373	39.4
Jewish	117	108	485	720	235	32.6
TOTAL BRIDES *[incl. misc.]*	4,696	6,368	662	11,928	5,567	46.7

Table II. ENDOGAMY AMONG KHARKOV ETHNIC GROUPS—1960

Nationality	Percentage Actually Entering Endogamous Marriage	Percentage Who Could Be Expected to Enter Endogamous Marriage by Chance	Ratio Column 1 to Column 2 *[Actual:Random]*
BRIDES			
Russian	46	39	1:2
Ukrainian	61	53	1:15
Jewish	67	5.6	11:9
BRIDEGROOMS			
Russian	47	40	1:25
Ukrainian	57	50	1:15
Jewish	73	6.0	12:2

Jews because they have a sense of group identity, though this sense may well be strengthened by consciousness of discrimination by the regime.

The high rate of Jewish endogamy is significant from a somewhat different point of view. It would appear that a very large proportion of children born of Jewish and non-Jewish parents in the Soviet Union are no longer counted as Jews in terms of official nationality identification, and probably not in terms of self-identification in many cases. As Kurman and Lebidinskii put it: "the overwhelming mass of those born from mixed marriages of Jews, Poles, Armenians and others with Russians or Ukrainians indicate themselves to the registration office when registering to have been born Russians and Ukrainians," identifying this phenomenon as part of the "process of drawing together of nations." Undoubtedly the official attitude expressed by these authors is a major factor inducing children of exogamous marriages to identify themselves as non-Jews. The authors use the phenomenon to explain the considerable excess of Jewish deaths over Jewish births (22 per cent in Kharkov in 1960), at a time when majority Slavic ethnic groups were showing a sharp natural increase: "On the other hand, those representatives of the national minorities who are dying, being almost all people of advanced age, are registered as Jews, Poles, Armenians and so forth."

At first glance the statement would seem to imply that when Jews are born they don't necessarily claim to be Jews, but when they die, they do. The actual implication is simply that older people tend to have stronger ethnic identification; as a result, there is a significant excess of the number dying over the number born in those national minorities which have a considerable proportion of exogamous marriages. Obviously, even the 32 per cent marriage rate of Jews outside their own group, would lead to an excess of at least 22 per cent in deaths over births if accompanied by the following circumstances: (1) a low urban birth rate; (2) identification of most children of exogamous marriages as non-Jews; (3) the persistence of the trend over a very long period.

We know that in fact exogamy among Kharkov Jews was very much lower a half century ago and earlier, when parents of those dying in 1960 were married. On the other hand, there is strong reason to suspect that the Jewish urban birth rate is very low indeed, quite possibly below the net reproduction ratio. As a result, the Soviet commentary mentioned above does not appear implausible. This analysis leads me to doubt that the Soviet Jewish population — that having any sense of ethnic identification — has increased since 1959. From the long-term point of view of preserving an identifiable Soviet Jewish community, this conclusion is discouraging. On the other hand, in terms of the immediate future, the evidence of group solidarity is very strong.

I TAKE this group solidarity as a point of departure in analyzing the role of anti-Semitism in Soviet foreign policy. After examining the extremely enlightening surveys of Soviet press reactions and Soviet political actions in Eastern Europe concerning Jews and Israel, particularly since the June 1967 war, I find little else to add factually. I want, therefore, merely to provide a slightly different emphasis.

There are several generally recognized factors in utilization of anti-Semitism as an instrument of Soviet foreign policy. First, the desire to extend Soviet influence among anti-Israel Arabs. Second, traditional anti-Semitism as it affects the actions of the Soviet decision-making elite itself; that is to say, the Soviet leaders' inherent anti-Semitism, whether conscious or subconscious. Third, utilization by this decision-making elite of anti-Semitism as a means of internal political manipulation; i.e., a scapegoating appeal to anti-Semitic prejudices among the masses designed to enhance support for the regime.

In my opinion, however, there are more fundamental reasons for Soviet utilization of anti-Semitism. If it were due only to the three factors enumerated above, one of two developments might be anticipated. First, the USSR might find the Arab cause a losing proposition, and cut its losses. Many observers expected this to happen after the fiasco of June 1967, which demonstrated how little effectiveness massive Soviet military aid to the U.A.R. and Syria had had. Rational policy makers—however Machiavellian—concerned wholly with enhancing Soviet objectives in the Middle East might have cut their losses or at least temporized; but the Soviet leaders did not. Instead, they not only replaced the arms the Arabs had lost, but stepped up Soviet diplomatic support to the Arab states.

Furthermore (as the documents we have considered clearly reveal), the Soviet regime accelerated an extremely severe campaign of anti-Semitic, anti-Israel and anti-Zionist propaganda and activity within the USSR and Eastern Europe. Realpolitik, even of the most ruthless variety, therefore, does not seem to be a sufficient explanation for Soviet use of anti-Semitism in its foreign policy. Thus we may contrast the Soviet position to that of, say, Communist China (which also vehemently supports anti-Israel Arabs) or that of Imperial Japan (which, as I recall, at least nominally supported the Palestinian Arab cause in the 1940's). Both of these powers, for rather different reasons, were pursuing wholly Machiavellian policies; i.e., they supported whichever side could best enhance their interests, with little concern for elements of justice involved in the Middle Eastern conflict. But precisely for this reason Imperial Japan or Communist China might have been induced to change sides when the balance of their interests changed, in sharp contrast to Soviet inflexibility.

A basic factor is the peculiar relation of anti-Semitism to the internal power balance in the Soviet bloc. The subject is extremely complicated; I have tried to deal with it (down to 1960) in *The Politics of Totalitarianism*, and can only present the outlines here, involving the intricacies of "Kremlinology." In fact, my own attention was first directed to anti-Semitism in the Communist elites when I discovered that their power struggles were inexplicable if one ignored that element. It is true that anti-Semitism has a long, tragic history among the peoples who make up the USSR (the dominant East Slavic groups and also some Moslem elements). One might expect, however, a diminution of mass prejudice as levels of education and material security increased, so that even a ruthless elite would find appeals to such prejudice less rewarding. It is true that the elite itself, so recently elevated from the masses, might be expected to share much of this prejudice. But one could expect it, too, to exhibit a certain mellowing as it became more secure. Instead, though there have been ebbs and flows, the chilling tide of officially sponsored anti-Semitism has not diminished for thirty years.

ACCORDING to my information, official (though secret) quotas for Jews in salient posts were established as early as 1942. Official anti-Semitism became overt in 1948 and increased at a catastrophic tempo through 1952. At that time many observers regarded the development as an idiosyncrasy of Stalin; he was indeed morbidly suspicious of Jews. Others pointed to the influence of particular henchmen of Stalin, such as Suslov and Malenkov. However, when some anti-Semitic campaigns in Eastern Europe continued for more than a year after Stalin's death, observers speculated that Molotov or other "hard-line" leaders were responsible. Then Molotov and Malenkov were ousted, but Khrushchev continued an intensive anti-Semitic campaign at home (marked by widely publicized executions of "speculators" with obviously Jewish names) and heightened anti-Israel policies abroad.

There was, indeed, a certain relaxation immediately after Khrushchev's ouster; Soviet publications even quoted Lenin on opposition to anti-Semitism. Beginning at least a year before the June 1967 war, however, the present leadership began an attack on Israel and its connections with "world Jewry" which exceeded even Khrushchev's campaign. For the first time a major Soviet handbook on the Middle East (by O. E. Tuganov of the Institute of World Economy and International Relations, published in January 1967) devoted major attention to Israel as the primary "neocolonial" force in the area. Since the June war, the anti-Semitic aspect of Soviet foreign policy has exceeded all previous bounds in both Eastern Europe and the Middle East. We have already examined much of this current propaganda, but one additional quotation from a recent Soviet pamphlet designed for wide distribution among young people (I. Belyaev, T. Kosesnichenko and E. Primakov, *Golub*) is useful to suggest the "amalgam" in which Soviet writers try to inculpate Israel, Eastern European "Zionists" and American Jews:

> It goes without saying that the connections of Russian Zionists with Russian anti-Semites were only an episode of that broad collaboration which took place between the arbitrator of Zionism and the arbitrator of imperialism. . . .

[67]

In the United States there are 218 national Jewish organizations. Their list take up 23 pages of the Jewish Yearbook.
Beyond this, there are 251 local Jewish federations, and in
addition various funds and special councils, whose list
takes up 12 pages. These organizations carry on various
forms of work in order to conduct Zionist propaganda. . . .
Not even speaking of the 218 Jewish periodical publications, the colossal propaganda machine of America pro-
vides priceless assistance to Zionism, publishing articles,
essays, and reports . . . Everyone knows about the colossal
sacrifices of the Jews during World War II. The Hitlerites
annihilated several million solely because they belonged to
the Jewish nationality. But, however paradoxical it sounds
at first glance [sic], the World Jewish Congress — still another Zionist organization — was founded in 1936 in collaboration with the Nazis.

It is true, of course, that Jews have been few in the Soviet elite
throughout the thirty-year period just described; most were liquidated during Stalin's Great Purge. A small but influential group led
a precarious existence in the higher reaches of the regime until the
Purge of 1948, but the relationship of anti-Semitism to the Communist power struggle was much more strongly influenced by the sali-
ence of Jews in the Eastern European satellite leadership. It is
probable that the Soviet regime would have experienced great
difficulty in effectively extending control over Poland, Czechoslovakia, Hungary and Rumania if it had not been for the highly trained
and indoctrinated Communists from these countries who had been
kept, so to speak, in reserve in the USSR throughout World War II.

A large proportion of these "Muscovites" were, by origin, Jews.
The reasons for this phenomenon are complex, arising partly from
the composition of Eastern European Communist parties during the
interwar period (as analyzed by R. V. Burks in *The Dynamics of Communism in Eastern Europe)* and partly from the fact that Jewish Communist leaders could rarely survive Nazi terrorism in their native
countries.

When the "Muscovites" — Jews and non-Jews — went back to their
respective countries to turn them into Soviet satellites, a power
struggle began with other Communist elites who had spent the war
period in underground activity rather than in the USSR. Reasons for
the clash included almost inevitable friction between elements with
such different experiences; the ruthless power orientation developed
among Communist leaders of all types during the Stalinist period;
and alignment of Eastern European Communists with individuals
covertly competing for power in the Soviet leadership, such as
Zhdanov, Suslov and Beria.

Initially these clashes may have had nothing to do with Jews as such or anti-Semitic prejudice. But men like Gottwald in Czechoslovakia found it expedient to denounce their "Muscovite" opponents (e.g. Slansky, Geminder) as Jews in order to capitalize on the anti-Semitism in their own countries. Other examples are Gomulka's attack on Jakub Berman in Poland (though Gomulka is himself somewhat vulnerable to anti-Semitic prejudice because of his Jewish wife) and Rajk's highly unsuccessful effort to use the same tactic against Rakosi in Hungary. In other words, the fact that there was an accidental correlation between "Muscovite" and Jewish identification led (given the unscrupulousness of the Communist elites involved) to the probably inevitable clash between "Muscovites" and "partisans" ("natives") taking on an anti-Semitic character.

AT the present moment the same unsavory process is continuing in Poland, with anti-Semitism utilized as a tool in the Communist power struggle brushing off on entirely uninvolved artists and intellectuals. (See especially Harald Lauen *Partisanen gegen "Zionisten" Osteuropa*, February 1969). As the process unfolded between 1948 and 1953 it had a feedback relation to the Soviet power struggle. As indicated earlier, Eastern European Communist leaders were aligned (more or less as proteges) with Soviet leaders, who were themselves engaged in a bitter struggle for Stalin's approval and ultimately for his succession. Consequently, vulnerability (whether to anti-Semitism or to other attacks) of satellite leaders led to vulnerability of their Soviet sponsors. Moreover, although none of the latter (Kaganovich was apparently uninvolved) were Jews, several were personally vulnerable to anti-Semitic attacks either because they were falsely rumored to be Jewish (Beria) or had Jewish wives (Voroshilov, Molotov, Andreev, possibly others). Since Stalin encouraged anti-Semitism, the line of attack was deadly while he lived, as evidenced by the widespread implications of the "Doctors' Plot." But anti-Semitism, once used as an instrument of political strife, tends to be addictive.

As noted above, the anti-Semitic aspects of Eastern European purges continued for months after Stalin's death, and has recently been revived. The use of anti-Semitism for reasons of expediency in the power struggle seems likely to continue for decades, until all persons with Jewish connections are so removed from political affairs that any identification of opponents as Jewish, or pro-Jewish, or Jewish-related becomes manifestly absurd. Therefore, although this cause for anti-Semitism in Soviet foreign policy is a long-term diminishing factor in the Communist bloc, it is one which will tend to affect Communist policy in Europe for a long time. (Asian Communist countries and Balkan areas like Yugoslavia and Albania are

quite unaffected by anti-Semitism since they have never had significant Jewish Communist elements.)

As a result, any Soviet-bloc Communist leader will hesitate to lay
himself open to the charge of pro-Jewishness by advocating friendlier policies toward Israel. Indeed, in some cases (Gomulka is a good
example) vulnerability to anti-Semitism may be one reason why a
Communist leader adopts a rigorously anti-Israel attitude. Conversely, Eastern European Communists with a margin of independence from Moscow may be friendlier to Israel precisely because their
own careers demonstrate their complete lack of a Jewish "taint." It
is probably no coincidence that Gheorgiu-Dej and his successors in
Rumania, who secured power by purging Anna Pauker and other
Jewish Communists, have gradually come to feel it safe to make
mutually profitable deals with Israel. Similarly, the Yugoslav Communist elite (which, since the death of Moshe Pyode has included no
Jews) has maintained a flexible policy towards Israel. Marshal Tito's
regime has sided with the Arabs as part of its effort to lead the "non-
aligned Third World" and at times has worked closely with the USSR
(especially in sending arms to the UAR and Syria in 1967); but Yugoslavia has shown no intransigence toward Israel.

A SECOND factor which I think is often over-
looked is the importance of the Jews as a resource for the Soviet
economy and technology. Just as the bloody purges of Jewish members of the Communist elites have tended to obscure the continuing
importance of anti-Semitism as a weapon in the power struggle, the
imposition of educational and occupational quotas, and other measures of anti-Semitic discrimination, have tended to obscure the continuing utility of highly skilled Jews to the Soviet system. While a
careful perusal of Soviet materials could doubtless enable us to enhance our statistical evaluation of the proportion of Jews in various
professions, even a superficial examination (such as I presented in
Ethnic Minorities in the Soviet Union, Erich Goldhagen, editor) shows
that Jews comprise something on the order of 5 to 10 per cent of the
highly skilled professional man (and woman) power which is the
Soviet Union's scarcest commodity.

The regime, therefore, simply cannot afford, economically or tech-
nologically, to dispense with the Jews' services. To some extent this
is true even of Communist Party membership and lower level implementation posts where Jews continue to constitute a much higher
proportion than in the general population: a decade ago, at least,
6 or 7 per cent in Byelorussia and the Ukraine, as against 1 to 2 per
cent of the population.

In all of these occupations Jews are (with rare exceptions) excluded from key decision-making positions, but they receive many material perquisites. To put it another way, the regime has a very definite though declining interest in holding the Jews as captive labor, performing relatively pleasant and highly remunerated tasks, but captives nonetheless in the sense that they must serve the system without participating in its decisions.

Obviously the regime's need acts as a bar to emigration of Jews, to Israel or elsewhere, unless they are no longer occupationally productive. This need may also act as a brake on the more frightful effects of anti-Semitism, though it appears that the regime is not averse to keeping its Jewish labor force in a state of uneasiness (the stick in the background has always been a major Soviet work incentive). But the regime's need to avoid a Jewish "brain drain" (mainly from the USSR itself, to a slight extent from Eastern European satellites) acts as another factor in its anti-Israel foreign policy.

The regime is no doubt aware of the Jewish ethnic solidarity which I endeavored to demonstrate earlier. If Jews within the USSR exhibit this solidarity, it is only natural to suppose that they would feel a solidarity with a dynamic, successful Jewish state. Consequently, Soviet policy has a strong incentive to restrict and humiliate Israel—but not to destroy it, since a weak, humiliated Israel could be used by Soviet propaganda to demonstrate to Soviet Jews that, after all, they had better accept their fate in the USSR.

IN this connection, it is important to recall that in 1948 the USSR was one of the prime proponents of Israel. Soviet representatives (together with American) secured passage of the United Nations resolution authorizing the formation of the State of Israel; the USSR rushed to recognize the new state; and Soviet agents dispatched a very substantial quantity of arms to Israel by air, in addition to recruiting and training Eastern European Jews for fighting in the Israeli forces. The history of these events was obscure for a long time, but now the Israel government is becoming quite relaxed about providing information on the topic (I have a Ph.D. candidate who is doing a dissertation on Soviet aid to Israel, using archives in Israel).

Important though they were for a brief period, Soviet aid measures were very transitory; essentially, support of Israel represented a "target of opportunity" for the Soviet regime. The motives seem to have been (1) a belief that the very widespread Jewish resentment against Western inaction while Nazis were annihilating Jews in Eastern Europe would lead to a prolonged anti-Western stance of Jews in Europe and Israel, and (2) a belief that in any case the foundation of Israel would create a prolonged chaos in the Middle East (probably the Soviet regime did not anticipate the rapid Israeli victory).

Since the Soviet Union had at that time practically no leverage in the Arab world to create disruptive forces in the Middle East, the "Israeli ploy" must have seemed temporarily attractive. But by 1949, when both of the beliefs turned out to be erroneous, Soviet policy shifted to a bitter anti-Israel position. The shift was probably accelerated by the discovery that Soviet Jews were impressed and gratified by the startling success of the State of Israel. The Soviet regime could not countenance the possibility of an outside force serving as an attraction for its captive Jewish labor force. Sweeping accusations against Israel demonstrated to the Soviet Jews that they had no hope of emigration or even maintenance of friendly contact with Israelis.

At the same time, murder by a staged "accident" of the leading Yiddish actor Solomon Mikhoels and covert execution of the Jewish Comintern leader S. A. Lozovsky, while possibly resulting directly from the power struggle, warned Jewish members of the elite that any identification with Jewish affairs was extremely dangerous. It is worth noting that even at the beginning of the effort to secure Jewish support for Soviet anti-Nazi war efforts (the formation of the NKVD-dominated Jewish Anti-Fascist Committee in 1941) a similar "Aesopian" warning was issued by the brutal execution of the democratic leaders of the Polish Jewish Bund, Henryk Alter and Wiktor Erlich.

THE third underlying factor is perhaps the most controversial and I advance it very tentatively. It relates to the nature of Leninism as a doctrine both monolithic in its claims and mass-oriented in its appeals.

To the monolithic concept of social control, any group which exhibits a strong sense of solidarity derived from sources extreneous to the monolithic ideology is suspect. As we have seen, the Jews of the Soviet Union have persistently maintained this sense of solidarity. Paradoxically, it may be precisely the Leninist assertion of monolithic control which has (along with the anti-Semitic factors discussed earlier) enhanced Jewish solidarity. For a major aspect of the Leninist drive toward monolithic social control is its emphasis on the masses of the people.

In the embryonic Soviet Union, these masses consisted primarily of the Slavic and Moslem rural populations, the "dark" submerged people of Tsarist days. In its appeal to them, together with its insistence on monolithic control, the Leninist doctrine acted as a mobilization ideology. The peasant masses were rapidly mobilized socially and politically, through urbanization, education and promotion to technically skilled jobs. In contrast to these masses were the diasporas of the old Tsarist Empire—Armenians, Germans and especially Jews—who, as urbanized and educated elements, already occupied a high proportion of skilled posts.

The extraordinarily rapid ascent of the Slavic and Moslem peasant strata displaced some diaspora holders of skilled positions. A more liberal regime might have reduced or eliminated this invidious development by making the largest and most privileged ethnic group, the urban Russians, pay part of the "costs" of the rise of the rural masses, or more simply (as has until recently been the principle in the United States) insisting on promotion wholly by individual merit. Instead, the regime (as Khrushchev himself implied) diverted the impatience of the socially ascendant elements against the Jews by limiting the latter's access to higher education and skilled posts, and indirectly by anti-Semitic propaganda.

It would not be fair to allege that Lenin's doctrine sanctioned this development. Lenin himself was sincerely opposed to anti-Semitism; even in recent years rare quotations from his writings on the subject have acted as the most powerful counter-tendency to anti-Semitism. There does, however, seem to be an inherent, unrecognized logic in Leninism which tends to sacrifice the small, dispersed minority to the "basic" ethnic mass. While (as far as I am aware) this principle has never been openly avowed in regard to the USSR, a recent Soviet work on the emergence of the Turkish Republic asserts that the elimination (often, in fact, by massacre) of the "compradore bourgeoisie" (mainly Armenian and Greek, but comparable as dispersed, urban, educated minorities to the Soviet diasporas) was a prime factor in strengthening the more "progressive" national bourgeoisie. (See my discussion in Kurt London, editor, *The Soviet Union: A Half Century of Communism*).

Insofar as they continue to adhere to Leninism, Communist regimes independent of Moscow are also affected by this bias against diasporas. One must recognize that, for all its amazing insights and sincere concern for progress, Leninist doctrine tends generally to inculcate a ruthless disregard for groups as well as individuals which the doctrine perceives as obstacles. In practice, however, Cuba, Albania, Yugoslavia and the Asian Communist regimes, having neither significant Jewish populations nor elite members vulnerable to anti-Semitic attack, have pursued anti-Israel policies on a purely expediential basis rather than as part of a far-reaching complex of foreign and domestic policy.

ALL three underlying factors which I have sketched above (and I want to emphasize that they are vastly more complex than my brief analysis indicates) suggest that Soviet foreign policy is more committed to a basically anti-Semitic position than would be anticipated merely from the residue of traditional anti-Semitism in the USSR, or from a pursuit of Machiavellian tactics designed to secure Arab support. The three factors — the role of anti-Semitism in the Communist power struggle, the desire to retain skilled captive labor and the general preference for mobilizing ethnic masses over diasporas — tend to lock the Soviet regime and its Eastern European satellites into a basically anti-Israel position in the Middle East and into manipulation of the Jewish question for political purposes within their own countries.

The link between the two aspects of anti-Semitic foreign policy is strong and vicious. If the USSR and its satellites did not have large Jewish minorities, the prospect of their adopting a more flexible policy toward Israel would be brighter. If, on the other hand, Israel did not exist it is possible that some of the anti-Semitic tendencies within the Soviet block would be moderated.

But (if our analysis is correct) the Soviet Jewish community, as a group conscious of its identity, is not going to disappear through assimilation — nor could one humanly desire such a "solution." Similarly, Israel is not going to disappear in order to "solve" the dilemma of Soviet anti-Semitic policies — particularly since, in the long run, the presence of Israel may turn out to be a saving factor for the Jews of Eastern Europe and the Soviet Union.

In the short run, however, given the value presuppositions of the totalitarian ethic, the Soviet regime seems obdurate in its opposition to Israel. It seems to me that anyone thinking about the way in which great-power relations, or indeed general international relations, can be carried out in regard to the Middle East, must take into account this fact. One cannot expect a set of concessions, a set of bargaining conditions, a *modus vivendi* reached with the USSR on the question of Israel and the Arab states to have the kind of operating principles and effects that a settlement reached even with a highly cynical and Machiavellian great power operating purely on the basis of its own interests might have. In dealing with the USSR on the Middle East, on the contrary, one must constantly be aware that the Soviet position is inflexibly anti-Israel.

What, then, are the prospects for the Jews of the USSR? The question is very similar to that put to me for two decades by my friends from Eastern Europe, particularly Ukrainians, but most recently Czechoslovaks.

For me, whose personal origins are remote from Eastern Europe, yet who for so long has been deeply involved in the area's problems in a professional and human sense, any response is agonizing. It would be quite out of place for me to suggest tactics or propose solutions. But I believe that I have one clear obligation: to tell the truth, as I see it, as completely and as bluntly as possible. If there is one failing—in divers quarters—which has debilitated our national life during the last few years, it has been the effort to paper over problems, to adopt a Pollyanna attitude until the debacle is upon us.

In my sphere of interest, this was most spectacularly true during the Czech crisis. I am not sure what a blunt appraisal by American commentators of the chances for Soviet intervention would have led the people involved to do; but I am utterly convinced that the Czechs had a moral right to such an appraisal by outside "experts." No wish, understandable as it might be, to close on an optimistic note would justify making a similar error of judgment concerning the prospects for Soviet Jewry.

The last thirty years have seen none but transitory ameliorations in the situation of the Soviet Jews; purely on the basis of extrapolation it would be rash to predict amelioration. Nor can one point to concrete evidence of trends which would, in the foreseeable future, lead to a better situation. It is true that the vast majority of the present leadership, trained under Stalin, is at an advanced age level, and must therefore inevitably disappear in the next decade. Conceivably their replacements will have more favorable attitudes toward their Jewish fellow citizens; but there is no concrete evidence that young men like Shelepin have different attitudes from their present associates.

I am indebted to Dr. William Korey for calling to my attention relevant data in a very recent Soviet publication, L. N. Terenteva, "Determination of Their National Identity in Youths in Nationally Mixed Families," *Sovetskaia Etnografiia*, No. 3, 1969. As the title indicates, the material relates to young persons stating their nationality on obtaining internal passports at the age of 16, and is therefore not strictly comparable to data on contemporary marriages.

Nevertheless, the data (from three major Baltic-area cities) suggest a picture very similar to that obtained from the Kharkov study. In both Vilnius and Riga, the proportion of Jews is slightly over 6 per cent, whereas Russians are somewhat over a third in the former city, about half in the latter. If marriages had been on a purely random basis, one would therefore expect (though the great population shifts over the extended time that the marriages took place make the calculation far less reliable than in the case of the *contemporary* Kharkov marriages) that the vast majority of the adolescents with a Jewish parent would also have a non-Jewish parent, and that about half of the latter would be Russians.

In fact, approximately four times as many Vilnius youths in this category had endogamous Jewish parents as had Russian-Jewish parents, and the ratio in Riga was about six times as many from endogamous Jewish as from Russian-Jewish families. On the other hand, an overwhelming proportion (some 90 per cent) of these adolescents who *did* have Russian and Jewish parents chose to identify themselves officially as Russian.

Less complete data from Tallinn suggests that this preponderance of Russian identification occurred regardless of whether the Russian parent was father or mother.

[75]

ANTI-SEMITISM AS AN INSTRUMENT OF SOVIET POLICY

ALEX INKELES

THESE remarks will focus primarily on the domestic aspects of Soviet anti-Semitism. As one surveys the racist and near-racist policies and sentiments allowed and encouraged by the Soviet Union, one can only feel a sense of helplessness and, indeed, of substantial despair. This despair is not even so much over the fate of Jews in the USSR—though that may become very much an issue—as it is over the spectacle of a powerful nation boasting rich cultural traditions and accomplishments openly espousing oppressive policies toward some minorities within its borders, the Jews being only one example. Soviet treatment of its Jews may be regarded as an indicator of policy drift within the Soviet Union and as a barometer of the degree of sanity in world affairs. It also poses a very deep and more general challenge, whose significance far overshadows the treatment accorded to any one minority.

Two general cautionary statements must serve as preface for specific discussion. First of all, for a true perspective on the present Soviet use of anti-Semitism, it is important to remember that the Soviet mass media have many times in the past mounted attacks on other objects, such as for example the Voice of America broadcasts, using basically the same means that they are now using against the Jews. The style of discourse, the specific terms, the cartoons, many of the slogans now apparent are, in other words, part of a pattern with a long history in Soviet mass communications. Although this cannot be any comfort, the treatment of the Jews is not unique; it springs from deep wells.

In addition, it is helpful to clarity of analysis to keep in mind that the use of anti-Semitism as a tool of policy is bound to have a different meaning in a country like the Soviet Union which—after the United States of America—has the largest Jewish minority in the world and one which is well diffused and plays a significant role in society than it has in a country like Poland, which now harbors only a miniscule and highly concentrated remnant of a Jewish community. Nor should one blanket all of Eastern Europe in the same analysis, Czechoslovakia having in this regard stood out as an exception among its neighbors.

With these general reservations in mind, let us move on to a few specific points concerning the connection between some present-day events and certain aspects of Soviet history, of East European history and of Communist social structure. First, one might stress that we are in part seeing in the anti-Semitic posture of these countries a reflection of the general tension felt in both the Soviet Union and Eastern Europe at large. And that general tension, which has in some cases become almost intolerable for the people involved, has in part spilled over into the Jewish question and into the question of Israel. The Soviet Union—especially in its relationship to Eastern Europe— and each of the East European Communist countries in their relationship to each other and to the Soviet Union, are facing a very profound political and social crisis. They are caught up in a process in which they clearly recognize the urgent need for moving from a Stalinist model with its exceptional internal and international rigidity to a system of greater flexibility and adaptability and one much more adjusted to the process of almost continuous change characteristic of modern industrial societies. This transition cannot be easily achieved anywhere; within the framework of a Soviet or Soviet-Communist system such a transition is extraordinarily difficult. Under such circumstances, any substitute for working out tensions and difficulties which cannot be easily handled in an open manner is likely to play an important role. Anti-Semitism plays such a role. There may, for example, as Professor Armstrong suggested earlier, be tensions between the various Soviet elites. One of these groups may be tempted to strengthen its position through the use of any available tool. It then becomes very difficult for the elite sub-group on the defensive to handle the resulting situation effectively or to resolve it.

Furthermore, in substantial degree, the nature of Communist ideology in the Stalinist and post-Stalinist eras has shown a strong, built-in tendency toward a type of prejudice which can easily slide over into "racial" thinking. Preoccupied with the existence of blocs and with a somewhat paranoid notion of conspiratorial activity; intent on the difficulties of handling diversity of opinion; assuming that individuals are most likely to be identified with what are broadly defined as class interests—a nation which may easily spill over into concepts of "racial interest" or "ethnic interest," Communist ideology encourages a propensity among those who have been trained in the system to a particular kind of intellectual shifting of gears. This "shifting of gears" may lead easily from those categories which are ordinarily defined in Marxist or post-Marxist terms into categories which are not ordinarily part of that system but which lend themselves to the same kind of reasoning. The shift from the concept of class interest to that of ethnic interest, mentioned above, would be one example in point.

ANOTHER specific point which should be kept in mind has to do with the processes, of relatively long standing in the Soviet Union and in Eastern Europe, which have played a substantial role in increasing the relative proportional weight within the Communist elites of a certain kind of intellectual from a certain kind of family and cultural tradition. Over the past twenty or thirty years, the Soviet Union has had one of the highest rates of social mobility in the world. This mobility has not only been associated with emphasis on education and the technical features of development. It has also involved opening remarkably large-scale channels of social mobility for individuals chosen mainly for their political loyalty, that is people who have come up through the party apparatus and other, similar channels.

With this system, the emphasized qualities have on the whole not been the sort one identifies with the humane tradition or with liberalism. Rather they have involved a narrow-minded, closed-minded, automatic kind of loyalty. Many have carried these traits with them to the top of the bureaucratic apparatus. Furthermore, in the process of so doing, many of them have, within one generation, moved over very wide ranges of the social hierarchy or scale without having an intervening experience either for themselves or by a generational gap of exposure to the broader and more liberal traditions of the Western philosophical orientation previously passed on within families and in the universities in Russia.

Under the circumstances, many of these people have carried with them into the higher reaches of the party and political apparatus feelings which are of the anti-Semitic type as well as general tendencies toward prejudice which are everywhere more widely diffused among those who have on the whole had less education and less opportunity for a wider range of social contact, and for a general liberalization of their attitudes and values.

[78]

Present Soviet anti-Semitism is in part a reflection of this long-term process in other parts of Eastern Europe. In other words the relative weight, or density, of men bearing a certain kind of cultural, political and social tradition in the Soviet elite is now quite different from what we would expect in a country at the level of general intellectual, ideological and scientific development reached in the Soviet Union.

Closely related is a point which has already been made by Professor Armstrong but one which ought to be seen as a separate point: this is the fact that, almost inevitably, when one deals with situations of prejudice a realistic element in such situations will be competition for relatively scarce resources. This is especially marked in the Soviet Union because of the number of people of Jewish origin and their propensity, as has been true in recent historical time in many other settings, to seek out opportunities for advanced education and to emphasize work in the professions, the sciences and similar fields. This has led to a situation in which many people, stimulated in general by Soviet policy which has decidely favored the minor nationalities, seek to improve their lot in life, but, on making such an effort, find that many of the desirable positions have already been occupied by Jews. Given a certain breadth of personality and understanding, one can absorb such a situation; but people who lack such qualities may find it difficult to do so. In an environment in which the government officially encourages anti-Semitic feelings, there are likely to be substantial outbreaks of anti-Semitism.

AN additional relevant point which has a long history in the Soviet Union and its analogue in the East European countries as well, is the difficulty these regimes have always had in handling questions of national identity in the sense of ethnic or other subroots; sub-national identities, in other words. The old idea of conflict between being a citizen of a particular country and being an internationalist, and the old slogan that the proletariat has no fatherland is meaningless, of course, and has been for about forty years in the Soviet Union and largely in Eastern Europe.

The problem has moved down one step. The real sticking point is that, within the framework of a Communist totalitarian system, with its demand for absolute commitment to Communist party policies, for individual shifting from one orientation to another if the policy line changes, and for the complete subordination in public of primordial individual identities if the national policy requires it, any group of the population which for either historical or other reasons has a relatively strong identity or consciousness is likely at some point to find itself in conflict with the central authorities.

[79]

The Jews are by no means, and have not been, alone in this respect. The people of the Tartar Republic have still not been restored to their lands or their general identity. People on the borders of China will soon experience very similar responses from the Soviet government if tensions with China increase. The problem has become so exacerbated in the case of the Jews, largely because of the emergence of the state of Israel and the increasing involvement of the Soviet government with the condition of the State of Israel vis a vis the Arab world.

This context automatically, under Soviet circumstances, creates a tension in which every Jew is, in the usual Soviet pattern, expected to declare himself publicly, vigorously, unambiguously as dissociating himself from everything which characterized him earlier and now vociferously identify openly, completely and publicly with the national interest as it is defined by the Communist party and its leadership. But under present circumstances, for the Jews of the Soviet Union to so identify themselves is extremely difficult: it is almost impossible. To the degree that they do not do so, however, they are identified as being "bad citizens" and therefore subject to punitive action.

Closely related to this is another issue which is manifested not only in the Soviet Union but elsewhere. In recent times, at least, there has been a tendency for Jewish intellectuals to show a marked tendency to commit themselves publicly on what they regard as fundamental moral, social, cultural and related issues. Perhaps this has always been a characteristic of the Jews, especially of Jewish intellectuals insofar as they existed. But it does seem to have become very marked in the period after Hitler, perhaps stimulated by the guilt or confusion that many Jews felt about the fact they had not been sufficiently active in their resistance to Hitler. Or perhaps there is a feeling that because of this experience they are more sensitive and more aware of these tendencies when they occur and therefore have a special obligation to denounce them.

But, in any event in the Soviet Union as well as in some other parts of the world and especially in other parts of Eastern Europe, there is a readiness on the part of some in the Jewish intellectual community to be rather zealous in committing oneself, in laying oneself "on the line" concerning fundamental public and social policy issues which involve human rights, censorship, intellectual expression and the right to align oneself with a group one feels a strong identity with. But the Soviet system has never had anything but the greatest intolerance for such attitudes. Soviet leaders have always tended to treat this type of response in an instantaneous, relatively automatic and really brutal way. In the post-Stalin era a certain degree of more public protest became possible; the resulting tensions have made those who make this kind of a commitment an extremely difficult group for the regime to handle, not merely with regard to Jewish questions, but with regard to any kind of public social or political issue. And for reasons which may be very complex and have nothing to do with proportions, Jews have figured significantly, if not necessarily in proportion outstandingly, in these groups. They have therefore become a target for the kind of tension and the kind of hostility which these regimes all feel in general and have felt in an intensified way under present circumstances.

THESE are some of the themes that are contributing to the expression in the Soviet Union at the present time of anti-Semitic tendencies. It is quite a separate question to ask what the consequences of present policies will be. Among the results one might include the following: In the first place, because there has been and continues to be substantial overt anti-Semitism in the Soviet and East European populations, those tendencies insofar as they are overt will now probably be largely legitimated because people will take the action of the regime as a signal of permission. And in many other cases, latent anti-Semitism will probably be substantially aroused.

Along with this, there is likely to be a tendency for public restrictions on the rights of Jews to hold certain types of office, to participate in certain types of educational institutions, to be functionaries of public bodies or agencies, to participate in international organizations in communication. In all of these areas we can expect increases in the number and form and in the intensity and the diffusion of the restrictions on the rights of Jews to engage in this kind of participation. These will rise in effectiveness.

Therefore, what has already become a severe problem will become a greatly exacerbated crisis of identity for the Jews in the USSR and Eastern Europe. Many who have for a long time felt that they could, in fact, resolve the crises of their participation in a society which they felt had only very weakly managed its tendencies toward internal anti-Semitism will now be having second thoughts. They will feel the regime's suspiciousness and will inevitably respond defensively to it. Among the defenses they are likely to undertake will be to consider somewhat more than they did in the past the possibility of leaving the Soviet Union, either to Israel or to some other place. To the extent that tendencies of this kind develop in fact, the regime will claim that what it has been arguing all along has clearly been proved; that Jews are inherently not reliable citizens, that they can never identify with these countries, that they always really had it in mind to go somewhere else.

And this is the kind of vicious cycle which is, of course, seen again and again in history, and which most individuals are rather powerless to prevent.

THE question of the relationship between the treatment of the Jews and other religious ethnic groups in the Soviet Union is a very large subject and one on which a substantial literature exists. I would merely like to point to a few relevant considerations. The most obvious, of course, is that the Jews are treated both as a religious and as an ethnic community. This means that campaigns against groups of "too much" ethnic nationalism and against religion both include the Jews.

In addition, as I mentioned earlier, by and large, Soviet ethnic groups which have some significant external reference of concern to the Soviet Union tend to be in relatively more frequent difficulty than groups which do not have that characteristic. In this connection, one may point to most of the people connected with the border states, or people of Germanic origin not in the border: they are seen as problems, in terms of Soviet international relations.

In this context one can say the following: In the first place, the reviling of Jews in terms of their religion is, I believe, not greater than that of other religious groups, as far as basic practices go. The Jews are either incorporated in blanket attacks or particular aspects of Jewish ceremony and belief are picked out in a way that does not exceed, in my estimation at least, the lack of humaneness or consideration for human feelings involved in attacks on specific religious practices of other groups. This is not to say that occasionally the attacks are not relatively horrendous and that in the case of Jews they may not arouse more special feeling because of historical connections associated with the ideas.

However, there is another aspect which must be considered and that is the gradual expunging of the substantial body of literature, of the theater, newspapers, dance groups and other forms of cultural expression which are specifically Jewish. In this case one can argue that the Jews in the Soviet Union have probably suffered more than any other ethnic group. Indeed, the basic Soviet policy has been to encourage the development of language, of dance groups and of other manifestations of local cultural identity *so long* as this was done in a way that minimized the possibility of, ultimately, arousing identification with the possibility of some independent or automonous political expression of ethnic identity.

However, in this the Jews share the condition of all other Soviet minorities not associated with a territorial political entity within the

Soviet Union. Census statistics and other relevant data show that the languages of ethnic groups identified with a territorial political region tend to be preserved or even spread and that the proportion of people identifying with such groups tends to rise. On the other hand, members of minorities lacking this territorial status tend much more to give up their language in favor of either the regional language or Russian; they tend also to identify more with a territorial ethnic unit.

In the case of the Jews this erosion has probably been more severe than with virtually any other group, certainly with any group of relatively or roughly comparable importance. But whether this is a result of Soviet policy or whether it should not also be in part attributed to the general tendency and interest of the Jews to in fact become absorbed and assimilated into the larger society seems to me a relatively open question; one which is quite complex.

Now this leaves one additional element: opportunity. This is a very mixed story throughout Soviet history. The non-European ethnic minorities have experienced a very substantial increment in their relative share of the national resources of honor, prestige, respect, education and information. This has inevitably meant some relative erosion of the Jewish position. On the whole, however, the change in the Jewish position has been shared by the Russians, the Ukrainians and other minorities of European orientation whose relative share has also decreased.

In fact, I do not think the Jews have undergone a decline in opportunities for education or for positions of responsibility and respect in Soviet society. On the contrary, they have shown a remarkably high rate of performance in both absolute and relative terms. The matter is really quite special and complex. Although there are unique attributes in the Jewish case, the treatment of the Jews falls within a pattern which is not absolutely distinctive for the Soviet Union. Obviously, no ethnic group is exactly like any other, which makes it rather difficult to say that there is really a general pattern which has been applied to the Jews equally with all others.

To sum up, both in the question of attack on specific religious practices and identification with an external political entity, the position of Jews has not been unique, although there are not many other groups in the same relative position. As for the loss of activities which help to define an ethnic identity, such as the availability of opportunities to use a distinctive language, to have a press, theater, schools which pursue their studies using this language, and so on, there the policy against the Jews has been quite distinctive and unmistakable in its relative effect: it has largely eliminated the existence of a Jewish community based on any substantial sharing of distinctive cultural attributes other than a general feeling or sentiment of communality and perhaps a religious component.

[83]

THERE are two critical questions to which I would like to turn very briefly. The first concerns the growing identity or non-identity of the Jewish community in the Soviet Union; the second, its response to its situation. On the whole, it seems to me, recent events in the Soviet Union have intensified the sense of community among many of the Jews in the Soviet Union who otherwise might not have had it. In fact, as we know history, this is not an unusual reaction. I believe the Jews are being subjected to a kind of terror and that therefore their situation is in a sense different from that of other nationalities in the Soviet Union. The Jews feel they are close to living in a condition of terror. I believe that is true. Almost all the reports I get suggest that. Every little thing that appears in the newspapers runs like fire through the Jewish community; its meaning is constantly explored by everyone and arouses profound anxieties for very obvious reasons.

One of the consequences of this situation can of course be the response that was reported to us by Professor Morgenthau about a certain segment of the Jewish community in Germany, and that is to deny one's identity more and more. The alternative response is to build a heightened identity. I believe the second response is taking place in the Soviety Union.

There is also a further question: what can outsiders do about the situation of the Jews. One should not of course exaggerate the situation: unlike many other national ethnic groups, the Jews have not been dispersed, their freedom of movement through the country has not been restricted; there are many things that could yet be done which have happened to other Soviet nationalities and which have not yet happened to the Jews, and there are no immediate signs of these things happening. But in any event, the situation is certainly serious enough.

I understand, and I deeply sympathize with, the motivation that leads people to believe there must be something we can do that would significantly affect the internal policy of the regime toward the Jews. I worry about this motivation somewhat, as this kind of American pragmatism applied to the political realm has led us into trouble. But I do think some leverages are available, of only modest influence. But they are leverages.

To start with, I do *not* think that what the United States says on the subject is likely to make very much difference. As a matter of fact, it is likely to be interpreted as still another example either of America's effort to do everything possible to embarrass the Soviet Union, or it will be taken as absolute proof of the great power of the Jews in the United States.

The sources of leverage, or rather of influence, on Soviet policy in this realm come mainly from three sources. One of these results from

[84]

the fact, I believe, that the Soviet leadership cannot be, and will not be, unresponsive to severe tensions in the Communist parties outside the East European bloc over issues of this kind. A real explosion in the French party, in the Italian party, concerning issues of this kind, do, I think, have a very substantial impact on Soviet thinking, although not necessarily powerful enough to bring about immediate changes in Soviet foreign policy.

Another source of influence of this kind which I think is very substantial lies in the non-aligned nations of the world, especially, for example, those in Europe, but also to an extent those among the developing countries. If many of them in their mass media and through influential sources and channels begin to indicate that they consider the Soviet Union a pariah nation because of its internal policy with regard to the Jews and other national and ethnic groups, this could have a very substantial effect.

And the third and perhaps less obvious source, but one which, I think, has to be considered, is that in certain ways the difficulties the Soviet Union is facing in reintegrating Eastern Europe in a looser alliance still basically under Soviet hegemony and influence if not absolute control, are greatly complicated by the fact that some of the Communist parties and leaderships, which would otherwise go along with the Soviet regime, balk at doing so because of its policy with regard to anti-Semitism and especially with regard to its insistence that that policy be imposed within the countries involved. This reaction could be a source of very substantial influence on the Soviet position.

All of these factors contain possibilities for influence on the Soviet Union. However, I want to emphasize that Soviet policy in the realm under discussion lies outside our capacity to make any significant difference in how the decision goes. Indeed the maximum influence we can exert, I think, would result from our maintaining a dispassionate and analytic attitude rather than from an attempt to create an environment in which we call for a "holy war" to prevent another kind of holy war from going its course.

THE JEWS AND SOVIET FOREIGN POLICY

HANS J. MORGENTHAU

PROFESSORS have a tendency to prove that what has happened was bound to happen, that it was inevitable, and produce reasons for that inevitability. If there were no anti-Semitism in the Soviet Union, if the outlawry of anti-Semitism, moral and legal, were then taken seriously in the Soviet Union, I could give you excellent reasons why this is inevitable on the basis of Marxist ideology, the classless society and what not.

Since there is obviously anti-Semitism, and since anti-Semitism is used as an instrument, a conscious instrument of the state, one is perfectly justified in trying to find out why this is so and what the factors are which make for this perhaps somewhat astonishing and certainly distressing development.

It has already been pointed out that there exists a residue of popular anti-Semitism in Eastern Europe which makes anti-Semitic arguments plausible because they meet the prejudices, the emotional preferences, of the population at large. However, the first objective reason why one might argue that anti-Semitism is inevitable not only in the Soviet Union but in any strictly totalitarian country seems to me to be the basic pretense of totalitarianism, and that is that it is the only source of truth and virtue available to a particular society. For this reason, it must be hostile to any religion not subservient to it.

NOW it has been since times immemorial the historic function of Jewry as a collectivity, as a spiritual and ethical and religious entity, to transcend any particular nation. It would certainly be an exaggeration to speak of dual loyalties in the modern political, civic sense but it is a historic fact that there exists within the Jewish tradition a moral and a religious loyalty which transcends the boundaries of any particular nation. A totalitarian hierarchy might not be consciously aware of this fact, but it is aware of it instinctively. It realizes that there is here a rival to its monopolistic claim to truth and virtue, and for the very sake of its survival it cannot condone such rivalry.

If you add the endemic anti-Semitic emotion which exists in Eastern Europe to this specific totalitarian inability to brook a rival in the monopolistic pretense to truth and virtue, you have a powerful existential element which makes for anti-Semitism in the Soviet Union.

Secondly, since the leaders of and the spokesmen for the Soviet Union deny that they are anti-Semitic, since they pay lip service to the moral and social unacceptability of anti-Semitism, they have in the existence of Israel and the relation between Israel and Zionism an excellent opportunity to mask their anti-Semitism. It is of course obvious that in the Polish and the Russian propaganda of recent times there are no open anti-Semitic references, but there is a continuous reference to Zionism. Zionism is the world conspiracy against which socialist countries must guard and of which Israel is the spearhead. Thus by proclaiming yourself to be anti-Zionist, you can at least maintain the pretense that you are not anti-Semitic. I remember I once met a member of the Saudi Arabian cabinet who invited me to visit Saudi Arabia. I was utterly unprepared for this generosity and I said to him, "I'm Jewish."

"We have nothing against Jews, we are only against Zionist," was his answer.

He took it for granted that I was not a Zionist, and he might even have been right. But in any event this subtle distinction allows one to continue paying lip service to anti-racial attitudes while at the same time practicing them.

Thirdly, the communist regimes throughout the world, and particularly in the Soviet Union, find themselves in a profound crisis: for since 1914 history has denied one after the other of the basic assumptions of Marxism. Thus, to an ever increasing extent, Russian Bolshevism has had to rely upon mythological explanations of reality joined with pragmatic success in order to maintain its pretense of its monopoly of truth and virtue. In our country a failure is not necessarily a failure of the regime. It does not of necessity reflect upon the political institutions themselves. The Vietnam war can be explained in terms of the personal mistakes of President Johnson. Of course; it can also be explained in terms of the overall inevitable tendencies of the social and political systems and the institutions. But in any event, we are intellectually and practically capable of separating the deficiencies of a particular ruling group from the deficiencies of the regime. In other words, the deficiencies of a particular ruling group do not necessarily damage the legitimacy of the regime.

But it is different in the Soviet Union. It is utterly implausible for the ordinary citizen in the Soviet Union to separate the excesses of Stalinism from the very structure of the regime, from the very nature of its institutions. It is impossible to explain that during most of the history of the communist regime in the Soviet Union this kind of personality, those excesses of a bloody tyrant, were a mere accident which had nothing to do with the regime itself.

So in the measure that the regime appears to be unable to live up to its assumption of a monopoly of truth and virtue and in the measure that in consequence the regime loses its ideological legitimacy — and there are obviously very few people in the Soviet Union who still really believe in the tenets of Marxism-Leninism — it has to rely upon pragmatic success in order to maintain and, if necessary, restore its legitimacy. Since those successes are very limited, both domestic and international, it must find an explanation for the lack of success, if not for outright failure.

The "fascist beasts," the "capitalist saboteurs," the "rightist" or the "leftist revisionists," the Trotskyites, and so forth — the Maoists now — have played this important, you may say, this indispensable social and political role. Of course, the Jews, the Jewish citizens of the Soviet Union, in particular, are predestined, as they have been in other countries, to play this role of being responsible for failure, or at least for the existence of internal and external enemies to the regime.

If you add the other two factors which I have mentioned, especially the existence of Israel as a visible, political incarnation of what the Jews seem to stand for within the Soviet context, to this one, you have a situation which indeed makes an active anti-Semitism inevitable, or at least it explains the existence of a virulent, active anti-Semitism.

HOWEVER, I don't think it follows that on the international scene anti-Semitism is bound to remain an inherent element of Soviet foreign policy. The attitude of the Soviet Union toward Israel has been extremely pragmatic. The Soviet Union was the first state to recognize Israel in 1948, and it supported Israel in the beginning. It became increasingly anti-Israel as a political and military vacuum developed in the Middle East, which the Soviet

Union could only hope to fill through establishing close relations with the Arabs. So in a sense, and I think a very important sense, the Soviet opposition to Israel is a function of the pro-Arab foreign policy of the Soviet Union.

One can well imagine a situation in which it might appear less desirable to the Soviet Union to have such close ties with, and more particularly to give such consistent support to, the Arab countries. If and when this should occur one can expect a different, more friendly, or at least less hostile attitude toward Israel. But what will remain is always the reservoir of anti-Semitic arguments which can be drawn upon for Machiavellian purposes, for purposes of power politics, domestic and international.

And I should say in this respect the situation of the Jews of the Soviet Union is at the moment, or perhaps even prospectively, worse than that of Jews elsewhere, but it is not essentially different.

Question: *Do you believe that protests and pressures from abroad can have a favorable impact on Soviet policy toward the Jews? Would it take some of the sting out of the argument that the Jews in the Soviet Union are somehow connected with the United States, if the organization and movement of protest on their behalf were international rather than American?*

Dr. Morgenthau: Let me take the last question first. I don't believe that the attitude and the policies of the rulers of the Soviet Union are susceptible to this kind of subtlety. I am pretty confident that their anti-Semitic vision is broad enough to take in all kinds of organizations, American or international.

Now, as to the first question, let me say briefly that the Soviet Union, both officially and as far as my private conversations are concerned, is extremely defensive about the accusation of anti-Semitism. They refuse to admit it. And I think any public exposure of anti-Semitism in the Soviet Union is bound to call forth a certain reaction on the part of the rulers of the Soviet Union. Private organizations, like this one, who point in a critical way to the existence of anti-Semitism in the Soviet Union have a chance to have, however small, an effect upon the practices of the Soviet Union. I think this has already been shown in certain minor ways, such as the production and distribution of matzos and so forth.

So I would not discard the expressions of public opinion both in the non-Communist and the Communist world outside the Soviet

Union as being insignificant. And I would even think that the expressions of opinion outside the Communist camp may well be more important than the others. For after all, it is an unfortunate and incontestable fact that, for instance, the revival of typical anti-Semitic propaganda and practices in Poland has been carried on with the support of large numbers, if not the overwhelming majority, of the Polish people. In other words, anti-Semitism is still a popular drawing card in Eastern Europe, hence, can still be politically useful, and therefore one cannot really rely upon dissension from this quarter to influence the Soviet Union.

As far as the actions of the American Government are concerned one is up against another basic fact of Soviet life, that is, the government's extreme sensitivity to interference in its domestic affairs. But on the other hand, one cannot dismiss public pressure on the part of the American Government out of hand as being unadvisable. I think one would have to look at this within the context of the concrete political situation. I could well imagine a political situation in which the Soviet Union would very much like to have the support of the United States or in which some basic interest of the United States and the Soviet Union coincide. Here a particular aspect of Soviet-American relations might be used for the positive purpose of improving the conditions of Soviet Jews.

So I would rather take an extremely pragmatic attitude towards this problem. I would look at the two horns of the Soviet dilemma: sensitivity to the accusation of anti-Semitism, on the one hand, and the fear of foreign intervention, on the other, and I would ask myself if I had something to do with American foreign policy, in each concrete instance: Is there an opening here? To what extent can I use the weakness of the Soviet Union in one respect for gaining some advantages in another?

COMMENTARY

MAURICE FRIEDBERG

THE Jews are known to be bilingual, trilingual — multilingual. Since the term "native tongue" is normally used to describe the language in which one has the most facility, it is reasonable to assume that in addition to those who consider Yiddish to be the language they speak most fluently, there must be quite a few Soviet Jews, as there are quite a few among us, who can read Yiddish, who speak it, or at the very least understand it, but who are nevertheless more fluent in another language and would therefore label that language their "native tongue." Thus, the number of Yiddish-speaking Jews in the USSR must certainly be much larger, perhaps twice as large, as the official figure of a half-million.

Furthermore, Soviet authorities would have us believe that the sole determinant of ethnic identity is language, and that linguistic assimilation brings with it a total loss of ethnic identity. We know that this is not so from pre-revolutionary history of Russia's Jews well before 1917, but there was no discernible loss of Jewish consciousness. In fact, it is only since 1917 that the Jews are permitted — or have been permitted — to retain a degree of "official" Jewish identity on condition that they use Yiddish as the vehicle for its expression. *Sovietish Heimland*, the sole journal published in Yiddish today, does print material of Jewish interest, but it also has such gems as *"A lied tsum khaver Lumumba"* ("A Poem for Comrade Lumumba"), sonnets in memory of Vladimir Ilyich Lenin and translations into Yiddish—believe it or not—of Soviet Russian verse. Now I wonder whether this is precisely what the Jewish *folksmassen* need. But it is what the editor, Comrade Vergelis, believes they ought to be given.

Before the Revolution, there was a significant body of Jewish culture in Russia in languages other than Yiddish. There was some Hebrew, although not very much. But Russian Jews had then at their disposal a magazine very much like the American *Commentary*. It was *Voskhod*; among its contributors were not only many Jewish writers but many Russian writers as well, including some famous ones. In other words, the loss or changeover in the linguistic medium was not accompanied by a loss of interest in Jewish life and in subjects of Jewish concern.

There was a body of profoundly Jewish literature, some of it preserved to this day, written in Russian. Is there anybody who would not consider Isaac Babel to be a quintessentially Jewish writer even though his medium was Russian? His concerns were Jewish. His protagonists were Jewish. His point of view was very much Jewish.

There were some lesser known ones, so-called ethnographic writers, people like Yushevich; or a man who is remembered today solely as a Zionist leader and publicist but who was once a reasonably well known Russian short story writer—Vladimar Jabotinsky.

In a recent issue of *Sovietish Heimland* there was a delightful vignette by Solomon Rabinovich of the Novosti Agency that told about his trip to the Georgian Republic. He describes a number of Jewish *shtetlach* in Georgia, which seems to be the only place where such villages still exist. There was one description which I found rather charming, considering that it was printed in a publication brought out in Moscow. Rabinovich attended the wedding of a prominent bemedaled Jewish engineer in Georgia and he noticed that the marriage ceremony was performed by no fewer than three *hahamim*, i.e., rabbis. He said to the engineer, in shock and dismay, "You have gone to a university. You're an educated man. What's the idea of having not only one rabbi, but three?" And he was told: "That's the way everybody does it in our country, Georgia."

So these pockets of intense Jewish life, even in religious terms, do exist.

I THINK it is of some interest to point out a dichotomy in Soviet geography between *provinces* and *center*. Geographically, the city of St. Petersburg was very much on the periphery of Russia. It was on the frontier with Finland; there were people who lived in St. Petersburg yet had suburban homes in Finland and were more or less regular commuters. Nevertheless, it was the old St. Petersburg — now Leningrad — which was the cultural capital of Russia.

But after 1917 an interesting phenomenon was to be observed in the USSR. The center of gravity of Russian cultural life began to move away from the two capitals, Moscow and St. Petersburg, into the provinces. And it is curious that one of these new cultural centers was also an established center of Jewish life in Russia — Odessa. There was a whole generation of writers that came out of Odessa: Isaac Babel, Yuri Olesha, Eduard Bagritsky, Valentin Katayev, the satirists Ilf and Petrov, and many others.

So it is not inconceivable that, just as in Russian literature in the 1920's it was the provincial part of Russia which influenced the center and not the other way around, something similar will be true of Soviet Jews in the 1960's.

As for the sense of Jewish identity, a good deal of it may be found in Russian literature, especially during the period discussed by Mr. Decter. During World War II much of it was written, particularly in verse, by highly assimilated Jews. You find poetry, profoundly Jewish in tone, written by a man as remote from things Jewish as the late Samuil Marshak, as well as verse by Ilya Ehrenberg. The poetess Marguerita Aliger quotes her mother as telling her, *"My-yevrei. Kak ty smela eta pozabyt?"* ("We are Jews, how dared you forget it?") And Aliger tells her mother that until the war she thought of herself as just a Soviet person, but now remembers that she is Jewish as well.

Analogous literature was written in the late 1950's during the post-Stalin thaw, particularly works set in the last years of Stalin's life. But to my mind the best proof of the existence of this sort of self-conscious feeling of Jewish identity is to be found not in the official but in the unofficial and the underground Russian literature. The reason it is underground is that, officially, Jewish consciousness, Jewish ethnic identity, simply does not exist. If it does not exist, it cannot be mentioned in literature. And underground Russian literature specializes in dealing with problems that exist in reality but not in theory — such as the crimes of Stalin, or the clash between the fathers and the sons, or feelings of cynicism and disenchantment and boredom with official ideology, or a desire to escape drab Soviet reality.

It is curious that the problem of the Russian Jew occupies one of the foremost places in the literature of the Russian underground. This, incidentally, is true both of writers who are themselves Jews and of those who are not. You will find scores of poems, short stories and even several novels that deal with it. Andrei Sinyavsky's *The Trial Begins*, Yuli Daniel's *This is Moscow Speaking*, Ivanov's *Is There Life on Mars?* and some of the poems of Iosif Brodsky, such as "The Jewish Cemetery Near Leningrad," are but a few examples.

IN the last year and a half—and particularly since the invasion of Czechoslovakia—the struggle against the survival or revival of Stalinism is always accompanied by protestations against the revival of anti-semitism in the Soviet Union and, conversely, whenever there is a crackdown on the dissidents in connection with some demonstration—such as protesting the invasion of Czechoslovakia—you hear the police and their aides shouting: "Beat the Jews. It's they who are stirring up all the trouble."

There is evidence of a definite tie-in between local nationalism and the degree of Jewish national consciousness in the recently published Chornovyl Papers in the Ukraine. There is similar evidence from other areas. People who are nationalistically inclined in the Ukraine would make it a point to encourage—within permissible limits—any sort of Jewish cultural expression because in this manner, indirectly, they strengthen their own case for more cultural facilities in their own language, for more attention to their own traditions, etc. This has also been true to a very significant extent—and overlooked too often—in Belorussia. Literary journals like *Polymya* and *Neman* publish much of this kind of material.

Jewish theatrical groups still travel to these far away areas, although not as often as they used to. The most famous Yiddish performer in the Soviet Union is no longer there. Nehama Lifschitz was the lone Yiddish singer available on records. She was allowed to emigrate and now lives in Israel. She has given concerts there and in America.

There is, of course, a possibility that with the departure from the Soviet Union of the more ethnically conscious and more culturally aware Jews, the remaining Jews will be deprived of leadership, of teachers, of impetus to survive as a community. This is inevitable. There was a process very similar in nature in Poland too.

SOMEBODY asked whether attempts are made to teach children any Jewish knowledge. We know from official Soviet sources that there are. *Sovietish Heimland* from time to time publishes the fact that parents with Yiddish-speaking children want to teach them to read Yiddish as well. Six months ago, instead of doing what normally should be done—print a Yiddish textbook—*Sovietish Heimland* began to feature in its last two pages a "teach yourself" Yiddish column. It appears at monthly intervals and it's pretty good—if you are an adult and know how to study languages by yourself.

The data on professional breakdown are available only from occasional press agency handouts which report that so many Jews are doctors, so many are lawyers, and so on. Incidentally, this is a bit misleading because on the scale of social prestige and income, the position of Soviet doctors and lawyers is pretty low. In the Soviet Union, medicine and law are often professions for women—considered a good second income.

Mr. Decter said he does not believe Soviet claims that there is no demand for Jewish schools in the USSR. Neither do I. There are several cities in the Soviet Union which are largely Jewish, and it is simply inconceivable that ten Jewish families could not be found in Moscow with its Jewish population of a half-million. In that major Jewish metropolis in the United States, Bloomington, Indiana, which is where I live, there is a Jewish school. In fact, we are now having a fight which may split the school in two, so that we will have two schools.

PROFESSOR INKELES mentioned the propaganda cartoons—and it is true that the State of Israel, Zionism and other Jewish themes are subjected to the same kind of treatment given Tito, who was once called a fascist hyena. But bear this factor in mind: whenever the Voice of America, or whatever, is under attack in a cartoon or in a *feuilleton*, the person, country or institution attacked has no counterpart in the Soviet Union. There is no American minority in the Soviet Union; the Russian announcers on VOA are invariably identified either as Nazi collaborators or as survivors of the *ancien regime* who found refuge in the United States.

The suspicion that these cartoons may have some domestic repercussions is borne out in a rather unexpected context by Ilya Ehrenburg in his memoirs. In the 1940's, or about '50-'51, there was a cartoon in *Krokodil* of the French writer, Andre Gide, labeling him a renegade from the Communist point of view. But the play on names, identifying Gide as *Zhid*, which means kike, created a furor in Moscow.

The connections between Soviet foreign relations and its treatment of its own minorities, are observable as with the treatment of the German minority. During the Soviet-Nazi honeymoon, the German minority on the Volga was treated exceptionally well; it was favored. When the Nazi-Soviet war broke out, it was deported *en masse* before any real charges of collaboration could be levied against any of the Volga Germans.

IN Professor Morgenthau's remarks, the point is made, quite justly, that the Jew is never attacked *qua* Jew, but a euphemism—Judaism or Zionism—is always used. I submit, however, that these are but thinly veiled anti-Semitic references, in spite of the fact that the Soviet sources often lean over backwards to prove that this is not the case.

For example, the Soviet Encyclopedia—*Boyshaya sovetskaya entsiklopediya*, second edition—is, to the best of my knowledge, the only source anywhere in which the definition of Judaism is given as a religion, monotheistic, most of whose adherents are Jews. I am still looking for the other adherents.

Now, to my mind, this serves only one purpose: it makes it possible for the Soviets to say that while every Jew is *potentially* an adherent of Judaism, which is a harmful religion, or worse still, of Zionism, a treasonable political activity, *some* Jews are innocent of such crimes. Thus, it is possible to make exception for the physicist, Landau, and for the violinist, Oistrakh. Which recalls the anti-Semitic mayor in pre-Hitler Vienna who was said to have declared on one occasion: "I am the one who decides who is a Jew and who isn't."

Epilogue: 1971

THE TERROR THAT FAILS

A Report on the Arrests and Trial of Soviet Jews

MOSHE DECTER

O N December 24, 1970, eleven persons stood at the dock in a court-room in Leningrad. Two were sentenced to death. Nine others were sentenced to prison terms ranging from four to fifteen years. The one woman among them, a young person of twenty-seven, was sentenced to ten years. A twelfth prisoner, her thirty-one-year-old brother, was tried separately by court martial ten days later and also sentenced to ten years in prison—all at hard labor and subsistence diet.

The world has never been apprised of the precise legal charges on which they were tried and condemned. Even the one or two Soviet press reports on the case never specified the articles of the Russian Criminal Code which presumably applied.

Nevertheless, on the basis of reports from relatives and friends of the prisoners, as well as a rather detailed summary of the trial smuggled out of the country, it was clear that at the heart of the case was an alleged plot to hijack an airplane from Leningrad airport in order to escape abroad.

Curiously enough, there is no specific Soviet law against hi-jacking. It appears, however, that the twelve, all but two of whom are Jews, were tried under three provisions of the Criminal Code the maximum penalty for whose violation was death: Articles 64, 72 and 93—as well as Article 15. We can only speculate on the specific rubric of each of these provisions which were made to apply:

Article 64: Treason—specifically "flight abroad" (presumably without permission).

Article 72: "Organizational activity aimed at the preparation or commission of especially dangerous crimes against the state . . ."

Article 93: "Stealing state or social property on an especially large scale . . ."

Article 15: Responsibility for Preparation of Crime and for attempted Crime—which assigns the same penalty for planning a crime as for its implementation.

But regardless of the legal specifications, the vagueness of the Soviet press, the secrecy of the actual trial, and the denials by Soviet propaganda organs abroad, the weight of substantial circumstantial evidence, filtered out of the country by thoroughly reliable sources, leaves little room for doubt that the thrust of the arrests and trials is anti-Jewish.

For these ten Jews (it is still entirely unclear how the two non-Jews became involved and what their role was) were among a total of thirty-four Soviet Jews arrested and held incommunicado—in Leningrad, Riga, Tbilisi and Kishinev—since June 15, 1970.

In the larger context of recent Soviet policy, it is clear that the immediate purpose of the arrests and trials is to stifle the voices of the many Jews who in the last year undertook an overt struggle to leave the USSR for Israel, where they can maintain their Jewish identity. The long-range objective is to crush a larger-scale renascent Jewish national consciousness among scores of thousands of Soviet Jews.

All the available information leads inexorably to the conclusion that in Spring, 1970 a high-level policy decision was made to undertake a nationally coordinated, concerted KGB (secret police) action against militant Jews. It employed entrapment and provocation and involved large-scale searches and seizures, confiscation of printed matter, interrogations and, ultimately, forced confessions that can be used as incriminating evidence.

The known facts are these:

At 8:30 A.M. on June 15, 1970, eight of the prisoners were apprehended at Leningrad's Smolny airport as they were walking from the terminal to an airplane. The remaining four had been arrested several hours earlier in a forest near a small airport at a town some distance from Leningrad where allegedly they were all to have assembled.

That afternoon, *Vecherny Leningrad,* the main afternoon paper, carried a brief announcement of the action, indicating that those arrested had planned to hijack the plane out of the country. The same item appeared the next day in *Leningradskaya Pravda,* the main morning newspaper.

The Soviet press, as a matter of policy, rarely publishes crime news, and even then it is not until long after the event. The fact that these papers carried this report within less than twenty-four hours suggests that they were alerted in advance.

The fact, indeed, that the Jews were arrested while walking on the tarmac is a sure sign of the KGB's advance information and planning.

The probability of a meticulously coordinated police provocation is enhanced even further by the virtual simultaneity of other actions that day.

At about the same hour of the arrests at Smolny Airport, eight Leningrad Jews were arrested in scattered places; at work, at home, on assignment some distance from the city, and even on vacation as far away as Odessa. Within a few hours searches were carried out in dozens of homes in Moscow, Leningrad, Riga and Kharkov; scores of people were detained for questioning and then released. Since June, there have been more arrests, in Tbilisi, Kishinev, Riga and again in Leningrad, bringing the number of Jewish political prisoners at this date to thirty-nine.

The man in charge of the Leningrad case, involving at least the prisoners from Riga and Leningrad itself, is the chief city prosecutor, S. Ye. Soloviov, well known to local Jews as an anti-Semite.

In 1961 he served as a judge in the city's criminal court and as such presided over two notorious trials involving Jews. In one case, he handed down a series of death sentences for alleged economic crimes to a group of Jews. In another, he sentenced Leningrad synagogue leaders, including one 84-year-old, to lengthy prison terms on charges of subversion—which actually reflected their determined efforts in behalf of Jewish religious observances and their active contacts with synagogue leaders in other cities.

I

These arrests, the December trial in Leningrad, and the ominous possibility of additional trials must be understood within the larger context of official policy, as reflected in the massive winter propaganda campaign against Israel, during January-March 1970. What began as a concerted nationwide chorus of condemnation of Israeli policies swiftly degenerated into a general anti-Jewish campaign. Publications in the thousands all over the country, through articles, editorials, pamphlets, letters to the editor, and caricatures, assumed an anti-Semitic tone and character.

The campaign itself was an expanded, but more intensified, version of the common Soviet propaganda line that now views Judaism as the ideological progenitor of Zionism, and Zionism as the equivalent of Nazism. The whole amalgam is a key element in the doctrine

[99]

of "International Zionism" as the Jewish ally and servant of Western imperialism — an updated and refurbished adaptation of the Tsarist "Protocols of the Elders of Zion".

A number of Jews, both prominent and obscure, were pressed into service in this campaign, to proclaim their undying loyalty, reiterate official apologetics about Soviet Jewry, sign attacks on Israel and world Jewry, and brand as betrayal the desire to leave for Israel. The apex was reached at a March 4 press conference in Moscow when 52 prominent Jews were brought by the Foreign Ministry to speak to the world and, indirectly, to Soviet Jews.

What must have shocked the authorities, however, was the instantaneous reaction of dozens of Soviet Jews, as individuals and in groups, in Moscow, Leningrad, Riga and elsewhere, repudiating the assertions of the "house-broken" Jews and their right to speak for all of Soviet Jewry. It was very likely in reaction to this unprecedented audacity that the regime decided to tighten their pressures.

Of course, the authorities have been aware for some time of the growing frustration and resentment of many Soviet Jews at the discrimination they face in higher education and employment, the widespread anti-Jewish propaganda, the hostility they and their children frequently encounter in the streets, at school, at work. They are also deprived of their cultural and religious rights, foreclosing the possibility of perpetuating their heritage and maintaining their group identity.

Furious with official anti-Semitism and inspired by the spiritual self-regeneration which Israel represents to them, a rising generation of young Soviet Jews rejects this situation as intolerable. Tens of thousands have applied for exit permits to emigrate to Israel. With few exceptions, their applications have been turned down time and again.

Several hundred of the more daring have circulated appeals and open letters addressed to the Soviet leadership, to the UN Human Rights Commission, to UN Secretary General U Thant, to the International Red Cross, and also to President Richard Nixon and Israeli Premier Golda Meir. In effect, they have appealed to public opinion and to the conscience of the world. Such letters have been written by individuals and by groups in every major Soviet urban center.

This wholly unanticipated upsurge of pride and national consciousness has manifestly so upset the regime that it has resorted to severely repressive measures. The striving for Jewish national identity has begun to be treated like a criminal or anti-social act, with procedures of intimidation used against many who applied for exit permits: interrogation by the KGB, expulsion from the Party, suspension from the university, discharge from employment, and general social hostility at work.

The final turn of the screw was the Leningrad trial.

[100]

II

As far as the Riga group is concerned, relatives and friends believe that they were entrapped by someone planted in their midst. Privy to their passionate desire to emigrate to Israel, and their repeatedly frustrated applications for exit permits, he gained their confidence by posing as a pilot and offering to fly them out of the country in the airplane he claimed he was normally scheduled to pilot on a routine domestic flight.

About the Leningrad group, we have learned in a letter from the wives, mothers and sisters of eight of them that police interrogators informed the women that the prisoners had confessed to anti-Soviet activity, and the attempted hijacking of a plane. The women made it clear that they believe these were forced confessions.

Forced confessions raise the ominous spectre of show trials. Such staged trials, using forced confessions as decisive evidence, are tragically no innovation in Soviet law and public life, even though they have been in disuse in the last few years. This sad tradition goes back to the early 1920's and culminates, of course, in Stalin's notorious Great Purges of 1936-40, with their anti-Jewish component. For Soviet Jews, this form of terror as an anti-Semitic expression began in earnest only after World War II, in the last five years of Stalin's death, known to them as "the Black Years." Those years witnessed a series of grim experiences: a massive anti-Semitic campaign of propaganda and purge against "unmasked cosmopolitans" (a thinly veiled and well-understood euphemism for Jewish intellectuals, large numbers of whom publicly "confessed" their sins); the liquidation of Jewish cultural institutions and the arrest and execution of hundreds of Jewish cultural leaders; the series of openly anti-Semitic show trials, replete with confessions, of the top leaderships of the Communist parties in the Soviet satellites (especially the infamous "Slansky trial" in Czechoslovakia plotted by Stalin in 1952.)

The wave of terror culminated with the announcement, in January 1953, of an alleged "plot" by which Jewish doctors had murdered, or were planning to murder, Soviet political leaders, at the behest of an international Jewish conspiracy in league with Western imperialism — a charge that is closely akin to the present Soviet trilogy of Judaism = Zionism = Nazism! Only the death of Stalin, in March 1953, ended what most observers believed was going to be a vast new purge, with an emphasis on trials and the deportation of Jews.

Lest it be thought, however, that the tradition was halted for Jews, it is essential to recall the experience and the lessons of the great economic crimes campaign of 1961-64 — years after the death of Stalin. This was another of those massive, nationally coordinated enterprises which the police authorities have staged so well. In this campaign all of the institutions of Soviet power were used to expose and eradicate those accused of alleged large-scale economic offense; such as theft of State property, embezzlement, dealing in foreign currency, counterfeiting, and bribery.

The Communist Party apparatus, the Komsomol (Young Communist League), the militia, the secret police, the regular police, local prosecutors and courts, and the national and regional press were brought into service. Crude propaganda material, overtly anti-Jewish, blanketed the country and mass trials were staged in which the accused invariably confessed abjectly and were given stiff penalties.

For the purposes of this campaign, the death penalty was reinstituted after a lapse of many years. Of the several hundred executed, more than fifty percent throughout the country were Jews — who constitute just over one percent of the total population. Just six years ago, the International Commission of Jurists, in a meticulously detailed study, pointed up the anti-Semitic taint of the campaign and certain Soviet Jurists themselves, in a moment of cautious criticism, noted its legal excesses.

More immediately and directly relevant to our present concern is the case of Boris Kochubiyevsky, the first of the Soviet Jewish political prisoners — a 33-year-old electronics engineer of Kiev, in the Ukraine. Kochubiyevsky was arrested in December 1968, and five months later he was tried and sentenced to three years of forced labor for "anti-Soviet slander." His "slander" consisted of a public defense of Israel in June 1967, his assertion in September 1968 that Babi Yar — the ravine outside Kiev where the Nazis slaughtered scores of thousands of Jews in 1941 — was a tragedy for the Jewish people. Also included were his statements, in a November 1968 letter to the Soviet leadership, that it was impossible for him to live as a Jew in the USSR since there are no Jewish educational, cultural or communal institutions, and that he consequently wanted to go to Israel.

In short, the accusations against Kochubiyevsky were essentially identical with the regime's real grievances against its present Jewish prisoners. His trial is now being viewed as a harbinger of gloom for additional trials, and as a foreboding precedent.

In the Kochubiyevsky case, Khronika, the generally reliable "Chronicle of Current Events" disseminated by the Soviet democratic underground, reported segments of the trial transcript as well as reports by persons present at the trial, which painted the following picture: some prosecution witnesses were provocateurs. Several repudiated the testimony they gave at the preliminary hearings; one admitted to having given his testimony while drunk; others said they testified under pressure from the KGB interrogators. The general public was kept away, while friends and relatives were not permitted inside the courtroom. At the same time, the KGB packed the court-room with its own members, as well as with citizens who were mobil-ized and instructed to act hostile to the defense. Witnesses were sent out of court immediately after their testimony, which is against Soviet legal procedures. The judge acted like a prosecutor, indulging in re-marks that were hostile to the defense in both tone and substance and generally permitting anti-Semitic and hooligan behavior in his court. At the same time, the defense counsel assumed the role of assistant prosecutor, not only accepting the basic validity of the charges against his client but actually indicating his disbelief of Kochubiyev-sky's own defense.

*   *   *

The Soviet authorities did, of course, attempt to underplay and even avoid the essentially anti-Jewish and political character of the Leningrad trial and of the whole "case" of the Jews arrested in these various cities, and have sought to divert attention to the narrow legal question of a hijacking plot or "anti-Soviet activities" (which include such things as learning Jewish history and the Hebrew language, and persistently and openly—and legally—appealing for exit permits to go to Israel). This would serve them especially well in a period of shock and revulsion against hijacking.

But it has been impossible for Soviet propaganda to shift the focus from the fact that people are on trial for their convictions, and that Jews are being persecuted as Jews. They had no desire to criticize, attack, change, subvert or overthrow the Soviet system. On the con-trary, their only desire was to leave that system altogether, and to exercise their elementary human right to leave their country of origin and settle in Israel, which they now regard as their ancestral home-land and as the sole place where they will be able to live as Jews.

The materials confiscated from those interrogated and arrested demonstrate conclusively that this is a Jewish case. Among the items seized were Hebrew grammars, Jewish history books, open letters of appeal for help to leave for Israel, postal cards from Israel, and Jewish encyclopedias. In short, as some have written, everything with the words "Jew," "Jewish," "Judaism" was confiscated.

Within days after the June 15 action, a young Leningrad Jew, Viktor Boguslavsky, wrote an impassioned letter to the Soviet Prosecutor-General, Rudenko, pleading the innocence of his arrested friends, noting that "A lively interest in the fate of one's people and love for one's people can not be considered an offense. Their only crime was that they were born Jews and they sought to remain Jews."

In July, Viktor Boguslavsky was arrested.

[103]

There can hardly be any doubt that, as a consequence of the massive and spontaneous outpouring of world protest—including condemnations from several Western Communist parties—against the death sentences, Moscow felt impelled to commute them to prison terms of fifteen years. A very significant lesson is to be learned from this development. And for the long haul, an even more profound lesson can be derived from the experience and reaction of the audacious Soviet Jews to the enormous pressures being brought against them.

On January 29, 1971, there arrived at Tel Aviv airport a young Jewish family from Moscow, the family of 32-year-old Boris Zuckerman. Zuckerman is a physicist who had in recent years made himself expert on the Soviet Constitution and laws. In that capacity, he served as a legal ideologist and advisor to both the Soviet democratic movement—including the Committee on Human Rights created by the famous physicist, Andrei Sakharov—and the groups of Zionists.

As he alighted from the plane that brought him from Europe, he declared:

"All the persecutions, the trial in Leningrad and those yet to come, have not frightened Soviet Jews nor led them into despair, nor weakened their determination to leave for Israel. On the contrary, all this has only strengthened their will. The movement, though not organized, is growing."

MOSCOW—CENTER AND EXPORTER OF ANTI-SEMITISM[1]

PAUL LENDVAI

THERE are at least three important reasons that make Soviet anti-Semitism a matter of legitimate concern.

1. Except for the Middle East, anti-Semitism as an official policy, as a witch-hunt which cost some Jews their lives and many more their freedom has, since the fall of the Third Reich, been found exclusively in Communist countries, the Soviet Union, Poland, Czechoslovakia, and, in a more distant past, in Rumania, Hungary, and East Germany. Since the exposure of the "Doctors' Plot," no top Soviet official or any major newspaper has found occasion to condemn the specifically anti-Jewish character of the case or to mount a mass educational program against racial prejudices. At his June 1967 press conference in New York, Premier Kosygin denied that anti-Semitism had ever existed in the Soviet Union. Quite apart from the fact that he himself apparently harbors anti-Semitic feelings of a rather vulgar nature,[2] there is convincing evidence of a *permanent* current of hostility toward the Jews in Soviet political life, veering between tolerated covert discrimination and deliberate encouragement of latent anti-Semitic prejudices.

---

[1] From *Anti-Semitism Without Jews* by Paul Lendvai. Copyright © 1971 by Paul Lendvai. Reprinted by permission of Doubleday & Company, Inc.

[2] At the Soviet-Czech summit meeting at Cierna on July 29, 1968, Kosygin insulted Frantisek Kriegel, a member of the Czechoslovak Party Presidium with the remark: "What is this Jew from Galicia doing here?" When Kriegel attempted to reply, Kosygin cut him short saying: "Shut your trap!" (Reported in the New York *Times* August 29 and confirmed by some Czech sources while others attributed the remark to the Ukrainian leader, Shelest.)

The question is not whether Stalin or Khrushchev or Brezhnev disliked Jews more or less, but whether they allowed the violation of one of the hallowed tenets of Marxist socialism which recognizes neither Jew, Moslem, nor Christian but only classes and class interests. While anti-Semitism in the Soviet Union as everywhere else has many and varied sources, the crucial point is that the operative logic of the Soviet system, doctrinal considerations, and, last but not least, coldly calculated "reasons of State" have led and still lead Soviet rulers to consider the Jews a security-risk group.

By its very nature, a totalitarian system cannot tolerate any form of ethnic, religious, or communal solidarity, any diversity of culture, any plurality of views or political currents. It must also create artificial outlets within the state for the dissatisfaction that inevitably develops.[3] The Jews, a unique minority with international traditions, a world-wide religion and emotional or cultural ties to their "co-religionists" beyond the borders (mainly in "hostile" countries) are a natural target.

But the troubled history of the Jews under Communism shows that the Jewish Question has never existed in a void; it must be viewed in the wider context of general policies. If it is true that the fate of Jewry has always been embedded in the structure of Soviet society, then the rekindling of latent anti-Semitism is a concomitant of the rise of social tensions in a conservative society which for a variety of reasons (loss of inner dynamism, evasion of major unsolved problems, a political vacuum at the top, the threat of China, and the growing strains in Eastern Europe) in periods of insecurity whips up party discipline and heroic traditions, nationalism and xenophobia, racialism and the hatred and fear of the alien.

It is not in spite but because of the nature of Soviet Communism that the technique of scapegoats, in this case anti-Semitism, is applied as a calculated device to release the tensions, conflicts, and struggles within the system. Recent developments in Soviet political life—the rising tide of chauvinism, militarism, and retrogression—have provided an additional stimulus to the emergence of the Soviet Union as the international center of an increasingly overt political anti-Semitism.[4]

---

[3] See for an analysis of the mechanism of the purge Z. K. Brzezinski, *The Permanent Purge* (Cambridge, Mass., 1956), pp. 12–37.

[4] Since this chapter was written, Soviet anti-Semitic and anti-Israeli propaganda has gained both in scope and intensity. In mid-1970 a new edition of Ivanov's book (*Beware: Zionism!*) was published, now with a printing of two hundred thousand copies! The author included new "evidence" of the "subversive activities of Zionist centers against the socialist countries," primarily Czechoslovakia. The Rothschilds are now accused of having financed not only "Israeli militarism" but also "the Czechoslovak counterrevolutionaries," the "West German neo-fascists," and the "Vatican." The French Rothschilds, for example, are said to have "financed directly the Czechoslovak counterrevolutionaries through a bank account in Tel Aviv" . . . (See extracts in English issued by the

2. Whether anti-Semitism as a political instrument is wielded surreptitiously with calculated moderation or openly with uncontrolled fury, under the conditions of a single-party system with a single dogma preached by Party and state, there is an important risk factor. "The fundamental reason for the superiority of totalitarian propaganda over the propaganda of other parties and movements is that its contents, for the members of the movement at any rate, is no longer an objective issue about which people may have opinions, but has become as real and untouchable an element in their lives as the rules of arithmetic."[5]

Communism is a world of manipulated myths which have often turned into deliberate policy what may have started as a casual misjudgment. The totalitarian state demands total loyalty from its citizens and excludes every other allegiance. The statements the leaders declare to be the doctrinal truth at any given moment must be accepted by their subjects. Thus the rulers must justify not only major policies, but the juggling of concepts, sudden changes in political tactics and in rhetoric (for instance, the alliance with Hitler and the carving-up of Poland, the ups and downs in the USSR's troubled relations with Yugoslavia, the switch from a pro-Israel to a pro-Arab position in the Middle East, the conflict with Communist China, etc.) in terms of sacred theory.

Both modern political anti-Semitism and Communism need an integrated belief system. This, in turn, possesses a logic of its own, leading inevitably to a conspiracy theory with absolutist trappings. Hannah Arendt has pointed out the decisive significance of the notion "objective enemy" for the functioning of totalitarian regimes: "He is never an individual whose dangerous thought must be pro-

Novosti agency and quoted in Le Monde (Paris), June 5, 1970, and Neue Zürcher Zeitung, June 11, 1970). Two anti-Semitic novels published in 1970 by the naval officer Iven Shevtsov have caused an international scandal and have been condemned even by the Komsomolskaya Pravda as "an illiterate, vicious, and banal collection of filth." Yet the newspaper of the Communist Party's Central Committee rejected the criticism of a novel "which contained nothing erroneous or contrary to reality." (See UPI from Moscow, April 27, 1970.) His first novel, In the Name of the Father and Son, published with a first printing of sixty-five thousand copies, speaks about the "international Zionist conspiracy" and describes "Trotsky alias Bronstein" as "a typical agent of Zionism, an international provocateur" unmasked in time by Stalin. His second novel, Love and Hatred, published by the Army Publishing House, enjoyed a first printing of two hundred thousand copies! The arch-villains bear obviously Jewish names, like Nahum Holtzer, the principal character who is a rapist and dope peddler who murdered his own mother, disemboweled her and wound her intestines around her head. Einstein is accused of having "stolen the relativity theory" from other (undisclosed) scientists and Trotsky of being implicated in the assassination attempt on Lenin by Fanya Kaplan. In the spring of 1970 an almost hysterical "hate campaign" was launched against Israel with mass meetings and the usual unanimous resolutions passed. At the same time, prominent Soviet Jews were forced to proclaim their hatred for Israel and their devotion to the Soviet Union, "their homeland assuring full equality for all national minorities" (Pravda, March 1, 1970). A number of Jews, seeking permission to emigrate to Israel, were reported to have been arrested in June and July 1970.

[5] Hannah Arendt, The Origins of Totalitarinism, 2d ed. enl. (New York, 1962), p. 363.

voked or whose past justifies suspicion, but a 'carrier of tendencies' like the carrier of a disease."[6] The entire history of the Communist movement is a line of plots, conspiracies, and treason, the ferreting out of imagined or potential enemies. Regardless of the forms of coercion and the techniques of terror (show trials and wholesale summary executions under Stalin, demotion, deportation, or imprisonment under his successors), this kind of system needs the purges, those "artificial revolutions" to release and absorb the strains within it, to preserve its inner dynamism.[7]

The need for self-preservation requires continuous self-justification since the subjects must profess unshakable faith in the infallibility of the leadership. In terms of the official state religion a Communist country cannot be imperialistic, territorial disputes cannot make enemies of two Communist countries, a Communist state cannot discriminate against a national minority, and such social problems as anti-Semitism and juvenile delinquency cannot exist in a Communist country. Since all those things do in fact occur, the official ideology has become meaningless and irrelevant to the basic issues facing the Communist regimes today. But it has not lost its operational effects on practical policies. It makes compromise between Communist governments difficult and often impossible since they are by definition "brothers" and must therefore conceal differences that would be considered perfectly natural among non-Communist countries.

At the same time unconditional loyalty to the "universal" truth that in any situation and at any given moment can be defined only by the dictator or the group in power has other consequences as well. Everything in a Communist society is linked together, so there must always be a mask of political respectability for a political practice that otherwise would seem shameful or intolerable. To put it crudely, stereotypes are sometimes more influential than reality, and words become deeds. Herein lies the enormous danger of systematic lying, which with the Damocles sword of terror is at the very core of a totalitarian system. "The consistency of fiction and the strictness of organization make it possible for the generalization eventually to survive the explosion of more specific lies . . ."[8]

Take, for example, the "Doctors' Plot." The case is now officially a "frame-up" fabricated by "despicable adventurers." Similarly, the 1952 trial of the former Secretary General of the Czechoslovak Communist Party, Rudolf Slansky, and his "Trotskyite-Titoist-Zionist

[6] Ibid., pp. 423–424.
[7] Brzezinski, p. 168. The term "artificial revolution" is from Michael Tatu's *Power in the Kremlin* (London, 1969).
[8] Arendt, p. 362.

center" was repudiated in 1963 as an invention from beginning to end. Yet fifteen years after the "fabrications" a strikingly similar "hate campaign" focuses attention on the espionage activities and political and ideological subversion engineered by "Zionism" against "the socialist countries." If we compare the hair-raising absurdities in the indictment at the Slansky trial or the web of inventions in connection with the "Doctors' Plot" with the recent spate of allegations about the omnipotent "international Zionist Corporation," an "invisible but huge and mighty empire of financiers and industrialists" created by "the blackest forces of world reaction" and acting as a "motor force" of imperialist efforts at world domination, we see the same spirit and the same methods.

Thus the erstwhile "murderers in white aprons" are innocent doctors; the murdered Slansky and his co-defendants are exonerated victims "of the violation of Socialist legality," but the rope with which they were hanged is being dangled again. Even the chief villains of Stalin's last script, the charitable organization Joint as the main instrument of espionage and subversion, and Zionism in the service of American intelligence, have re-emerged, and Communist "experts" on Judaism and Zionism use almost verbatim quotes from the source material prepared for the Slansky trial and the "Doctors' Plot." To be sure, there have been some minor changes with some alleged foes now dropped and new "objective enemies" discovered according to the changed circumstances. The "Trotskyite" danger is too obsolete a notion to be credible, and the "Titoist" conspiracy is said to have been "fabricated" by "Beria and others." These "outs" of the old script have now been replaced by new "ins," such as the previous collusion between Zionists and Nazis which has culminated in the present alliance between Zionism (which is said to have "all the characteristic attributes of Fascism"!) and the German "revanchists and militarists."

Many of the updated legends about the "Zionist" world conspiracy are so remote from reality that some Western observers tend to dismiss the Soviet diatribes as crude excesses of everyday political propaganda. One may recall, however, the notorious "Protocols of the Elders of Zion" which purported to reveal the text of twenty-four lectures delivered at a secret meeting of world Jewry. This blatant forgery prepared at the turn of the century by agents of the Tsarist secret police alleged that the "Elders of Zion" sought to foment wars, discontent, and chaos, to infect people with frightful diseases and to use subway stations to blow up modern cities in order to bring about a messianic age in which Jews would rule the world.[9] Following its publication in the wake of World War

[9] See Norman Cohn, *Warrant for Genocide* (New York, 1967), and J. S. Curtiss, *The Protocols of Zion* (New York, 1942).

I—not so very long ago—this collection of phantasmagoria became one of the most widely read books in the world.

Soviet tales of the invisible but all-powerful world Zionist conspiracy have the odor of the "Protocols" and were born in the same underworld, "where pathological fantasies disguised as ideas are churned out by crooks and half-educated fanatics for the benefit of the ignorant and superstitious."[10] Lest this comparison seem too harsh, let us glance at a typical Soviet article on the subject. The author Y. Yevseyev, a Candidate of the Historical Sciences (the second most prestigious scholarly qualification in the Soviet Union), stated flatly on October 4, 1967: "The number of Zionism's adherents in the United States alone comes to 20 to 25 million. There are Jews and non-Jews among them. They belong to the associations, organizations, and societies that play the greatest role in American economy, politics, culture, and science. Zionist lawyers comprise about 70 percent of all the American lawyers; physicists, including those engaged in secret work on the preparation of weapons for mass destruction, 69 percent, and industrialists more than 43 percent. The adherents of Zionism among American Jews own 80 percent of the local and international information agencies. In addition, about 56 percent of the big publishing houses serve the aims of the Zionists."[11]

Thus not only all of America's six million Jews (less than 3 percent of the total population) but also nineteen million other Americans are Zionists, and together they practically control the United States. The fact that these "statistics" were patent forgeries, borrowed from an obscure Egyptian pamphlet (published ten years earlier and probably ghost-written by a Nazi fugitive)[12] and "improved" by the Soviet author, was irrelevant for propaganda purposes. What matters is that they fit a new political situation. The fact that refurbished "classical," Nazi or Stalinist anti-Semitic myths are freely used today is politically more important than the fact that most of them are gross falsehoods. It is not within our scope to explore the details of Soviet "anti-Zionist" campaigns.[13] It is enough to stress that statements like Yevseyev's do not represent idiosyncratic views of individuals but rather the basic thrust of the state's entire propaganda apparatus, which constantly focuses the attention of the citizen on external dangers (American "imperialism," West German "revanchism," Chinese "great power chauvinism," etc.) and since 1967 has harked with ominous frequency on the threat of the "international Zionist conspiracy."

[10] Cohn.
[11] *Komsomolskaya Pravda*, October 4, 1967.
[12] See *Jews in Eastern Europe*, London, March 1968, pp. 7–13.
[13] This is done meticulously and reliably by such periodicals as *Jews in Eastern Europe* (London) and other specialized publications.

This is not to say that the nightmare of 1952–53 is again hovering over the three million Jews in the Soviet Union. But Arthur Koestler's perceptive insight into the Soviet system is as valid today as it was almost two decades ago: "They believe everything they can prove, and they can prove everything they believe."[14] The stubbornness with which the Soviet propaganda continues to cling to its lies about the Joint, Jewish finance, and the global Zionist plot, which were earlier repudiated by the same regime as "fabrications," compels us to reassess old assumptions about the "Black Years" of Soviet Jewry and about the temporary or incidental character of anti-Semitism as a political weapon.

We tend to forget that even in the age of spaceships totalitarian propaganda by its very nature must strive to fit selected elements of reality into another, entirely fictitious world. "Once these propaganda slogans are integrated into a 'living organization' they cannot be safely eliminated without wrecking the whole structure. The assumption of a Jewish world conspiracy was transformed by totalitarian propaganda from an objective, arguable matter into the chief element of Nazi reality; the point was that the Nazis *acted* as though the world were dominated by the Jews and needed a counterconspiracy to defend itself."[15] Similarly, the Soviet system, striving to keep itself pure of hostile contamination, manufactures dangers that become facts of life for the population.

Under these conditions, there is no effective defense or counteraction against such practices as anti-Semitism, for the ruling regimes maintain that these ills do not and cannot exist. Consequently, critics are almost automatially regarded as petty-bourgeois troublemakers who have fallen prey to foreign ideological penetration. If they persist, they are treated as potential foes who "objectively" act as the accomplices of hostile external forces.

In sum, the very fact that anti-Judaism or anti-Zionism must be presented in impeccable "Marxist-Leninist" terms as something completely different from anti-Semitism forces Soviet propaganda to dress up the essentially unchanged legend of a world-wide Jewish "plot" in orthodox ideology. The corporate Jew becomes a corporate "Zionist" (occasionally also a "rootless cosmopolitan") who stands for corporate imperialism. The practical and semantic difficulties involved lend an added stimulus to the independent force of ideological rhetoric, which in turn possesses a dynamism of its own. Regardless of top-level intentions, in certain historic situations the fantasies produced by systematic lying may become a political

[14] From his novel *The Age of Longing.*
[15] Arendt, p. 362.

force that sweeps along a divided leadership worn out by living in a constant state of crisis. This, then, is another extremely serious risk factor. The massive and incessant "anti-Zionist" propaganda has gradually constructed a theoretical basis that is in some ways worse and more coherent than even the pathological fabrications of the Stalin era. There is more than ample evidence that the Soviet Union has bred a climate ominously propitious for institutionalized and virulent racial discrimination.

3. Finally, ever since late 1948, the Kremlin, for different reasons and to varying degrees, has engaged in the export of covert or overt anti-Semitism. In addition to the dual threat posed to the survival of Israel and the position of the Jewish community in the Soviet Union itself, there is this third dimension of Soviet policy toward the Jews. And it is this export of first anti-Zionism and later anti-Semitism that has had a major impact on the fate of Jewry in Eastern Europe with which our study is primarily concerned.

One can distinguish two major phases in Soviet influence on the Jewish Question in Eastern Europe. The first phase (1948–53) coincided with Stalin's lifetime, when a single political system with a single line and a single discipline was imposed on the entire Soviet sphere of influence. During this phase of uniformity the position of Jewish communities was intimately connected with Soviet policy toward the Jews and in particular with regard to Israel. The Soviet Union and the United States were the midwives at the birth of the State of Israel, Stalin having decided that military and political support of the Israelis would undermine British influence in the Middle East. Then, on September 21, 1948, Ilya Ehrenburg's famous anti-Zionist article in *Pravda* heralded an abrupt change of line. In accordance with the traditional Bolshevik view, Zionism became a heresy throughout the Soviet sphere of influence. It was not so much the "ingratitude" of Israel—that is, its alignment with "imperialism"—but the emotional upsurge among Soviet Jewry, raising the suspicion of a rival allegiance, that tipped the scales and convinced Stalin that the Jews were an unstable, unreliable element. The targets of the attacks were first the real Zionists, then "the people without a fatherland" or "rootless cosmopolitans," and finally the faithful but Jewish servants of the Kremlin. The campaigns culminated in the Slansky trial, and we know now from several unimpeachable sources to what extent Stalin's agents were directly responsible for the witch-hunt that subsequently threatened the life and liberty of thousands of East European Jews.

Nothing could illustrate the irony of changing historical situations better than the fact that the same regime that had saved the life of countless Jews in the closing stages of World War II, only